HOW TO SELL
AT PRICES
HIGHER
THAN YOUR
COMPETITORS

HOW TO SELL AT PRICES HIGHER THAN YOUR COMPETITORS

The Complete Book On How To Make Your Prices Stick

Lawrence L. Steinmetz, Ph.D.

Published by:
Horizon Publications, Inc.
3333 Iris Avenue
Boulder, Colorado 80301
(303) 442-8114
(800) 323-2835
fax (303) 442-2803

For information contact Horizon Publications, Inc., 3333 Iris Ave., Boulder, Colorado 80301, (303) 442-8114, (800) 323-2835, fax (303) 442-2803.

Cover Design: Debbie Munshower
Text Design: Beth Steinmetz
Art Work: Debbie Munshower
Copy Editor: Sally Steinmetz
Composition: Horizon Publications, Inc.
Printed in the United States of America.

Library of Congress Cataloging in Publication Data

Steinmetz, Lawrence L.
　　　HOW TO SELL AT PRICES HIGHER THAN YOUR COMPETITORS.

　　　　　　　1. Sales　　　2. Marketing　　　3. Success　　　4. Business　　　I. Title
ISBN:　0-9631923-0-2

DEDICATION

To my children - Susan, Brad and Marcy.

ACKNOWLEDGEMENTS

There are several people whose efforts have helped me produce this book. One such person is my wife, Sally, who bore the brunt of my irritability in trying to get this book as right as we could make it. Sally is not only a professional editor of business publications, but is very knowledgeable in business practices and served more than anyone else in that thankless task of being devil's advocate, raising eyebrows, scratching nasty notes and question marks in borders of the draft manuscripts, etc. Most of the good in this book she helped get there; most of the bad is in there probably because sometimes I overrode her advice.

The second person to whom I owe a great deal for the production of this book is my most efficient assistant, Charlotte Buck. Charlotte has worked with me now some 17 years and has suffered through the thick and thin throughout the years. This is not the first manuscript -- not even close to the first manuscript -- that she has typed and retyped repeatedly. Surely, however, this is the most aggravating -- the reason lying in the way this book was developed. Rather than use my usual style of dictating chapter by chapter, I decided to try to make this book as much as possible like my seminars on the subject. Consequently, I started with a tape recording of my public presentations. Well, I discovered that you *can* write a book that way -- or at least start to write a book that way - but it certainly isn't the same -- and I'll never ask anyone to help me try to write a future book using this method. I never received even the slightest complaint or whimper from Charlotte for the *additional* retypings, reediting, and reworking necessitated by writing in this manner and I truly thank her for her assistance, patience and forebearance. I think it is truly a better book because we did it this way, but I could never have done it without Char's patience and assistance.

Three other people who deserve particular acknowledgement for their help are Debbie Munshower, Susan Wojciechowski, and Beth Kasten. They all spent hours in the mechanical design and format production of this book. I'm very pleased with the results and I think it is a wonderful tribute to their talents.

I must also acknowledge a few other people who had impact and influence on me in the production of this manuscript. Specifically they are the members of my Executive Councils -- a group of men and women, some of whom have been in my Councils for more than a decade, who repeatedly give me insight into how they manage to successfully sell products and services at prices often significantly higher than their competitors. It is very difficult for me to

ACKNOWLEDGEMENTS

pinpoint the hundreds of professional perspectives they have given me over the many years relative to the content of this book. I'll not single out any one of them as being "the best" contributor to my ideas because each, in their own way, have been the best. But to those who have been in my Executive Councils, I'd like to offer a hearty "thank you" for each and every one of their singular contributions.

CONTENTS

INTRODUCTION

Larry Steinmetz has hit a homerun with HOW TO SELL AT PRICES HIGHER THAN YOUR COMPETITORS - THE COMPLETE WORK ON HOW TO MAKE YOUR PRICES STICK. This book addresses the most common, nagging, persistent and consistent problem faced by virtually every salesperson in the world. . . . "Your price is too high," and it addresses it in a way that will empower the reader to deal with it in tangible, powerful ways.

For the first time we have an intelligent, penetrating and all-encompassing treatment of this topic. This magnificent book deals with all of the why's, what's and how's of this tough, universal challenge.

It makes no difference whether you sell a product, a service, a commodity, a big ticket, a demand or a non-demand product, this book is an absolute must for your professional growth.

I have personally known, followed and admired Larry Steinmetz's work for years. Well grounded in theory, his ideas have also been honed on the unforgiving anvil of experience. His ideas are powerful, proven, practical and productive.

After personally delivering well over one thousand seminars, conducting innumerable consulting assignments and in leading a staggering number of workshops, I have listened to literally thousands of sales professionals bemoan the inevitable pain that they must endure as they fight the "you're the highest price" syndrome. This book not only tackles the "how to's" in magnificent detail, but also explains the reasons behind and philosophical underpinnings of dealing with price.

I would like to congratulate you on your decision to invest your time and energy into this book. That decision could well be the single best decision that you will ever make in your professional career.

Very few books deal with this critical topic. None have ever dealt with it in such a substantive, meaninful and practical way. Read on! It will be well worth your effort. In fact, I guarantee that the ideas in this book are the most powerful, effective and eye opening that you will likely ever encounter.

William T. Brooks, CSP, CPAE
Greensboro, N.C.

FOREWORD 1

As I look over my personal library of several hundred books and audio cassettes, it amazes me at how much information I've accumulated in the past twenty-plus years. Searching the titles for patterns, I see motivational titles, self-help "how to" books, biographies and texts ranging from Buckminster Fuller to Peter Drucker.

What I do NOT see is many books I have read more than once. The book before you is one of the rare exceptions. It may take a dozen readings for me to fully learn all the lessons in this volume. And I'll continue to enjoy every reading moment.

Larry Steinmetz is a highly educated man (Ph.D.) with a gift for no-nonsense communication. In an easily readable and down-to-earth style, he leads you to expanding levels of awareness which cause the reader to speak aloud, "Wow, I didn't know that!"

When you finish your first reading, you will be a more astute business person, a better financial manager and a more effective decision maker. You'll notice things which never caught your eye before and be able to offer valuable, even critically important advice to your friends and colleagues.

Moreover, you will join the ranks of those elite few who truly realize how business works. You'll not only know what the problems are, you'll know what to do about them.

So, sit back and enjoy. Don't expect this to be "work." Let it become a straight-from-the-shoulder chat between you and Larry Steinmetz. Now smile, turn the page and get ready to say, "Wow! I didn't know that!"

Jim Cathcart, CSP, CPAE
Author, RELATIONSHIP SELLING
La Jolla, California

FOREWORD 2

HOW TO SELL AT PRICES HIGHER THAN YOUR COMPETITORS may be one of the most pertinent books of our time. Larry Steinmetz, in publishing this book, has really put his finger on one of the most difficult problems which face United States businesses and industries today.

For the past several decades, U.S. businesses have preoccupied themselves with maintaining market share -- virtually at any expense. In the late 1950s and early 1960s, General Motors Corporation dominated the U.S. automobile industries, having nearly two-thirds of the entire United States market. In the late 1950s and early 1960s, it seemed that General Motors' major concern was the possibility that the Federal government would attempt to dismember it because of its near monopolistic position in the marketplace. Market share was the goal of virtually all corporations at that time and most of the graduate schools of business in the United States were pumping out blather that those companies with the largest market share always made the most money, etc., etc. An oft-quoted statement was "As goes General Motors, so goes the nation."

Well, today, we see that the pricing practices and strategies designed to maintain market share has had an incredibly destructive force in our society. General Motors no longer dominates the U.S. automobile market, being reduced to having barely over one-third of the U.S. automobile market and, at the time of this writing, has lost so much money that it's operating loss in 1990 exceeded the gross sales of all but the top 214 largest industrial firms in the United States. Certainly Larry makes the point very evident that market share does not, by any stretch of the imagination, assure success or even profitability in a firm. Today's learned business journals, in fact, predict clearly the possibility of General Motors becoming another one of those corporate failures cited in Larry's book.

I teach negotiation skills and strategies. In writing my book, YOU CAN GET ANYTHING YOU WANT, I delved deeply into the process of buying and selling products, services and commodities from both sides of the negotiating table. I think Larry Steinmetz has put together one of the most powerful, pertinent and practical pieces of literature heretofore developed on the subject of selling products and services at premuim priices in a difficult marketplace. You will find his words on developing your competitive edge most useful in determining that niche in which you can establish your competitive advantage in selling. More importantly, you'll find his discussion as to the things that buyers really need and want in a purchase decision a basic insight into the truth of the fact that customers really do not buy on price and that the successful sales rep not only knows that fact intrinsicly, but uses it in commanding premium prices in the marketplace.

For those sales personnel who have not really had adequate basic training in the economics of pricing, Larry's chapters on how to calculate the volume swings associated with either cutting or raising price is an invaluable work. Sales managers and marketing executives should make those chapters an absolute "must" reading for even seasoned veterans.

Another section of this book which is immeasurably important to the sales person in the marketplace are the chapters on indicators of overpricing and underpricing. This section of the book just crawls with common sense and I've never seen anything so cogent or pragmatic assembled in such a useful form for the practitioner. These ideas are only surpassed by the superb presentation by Larry on the various tricks and tactics that purchasing and buying people use to successfully whittle away at the seller's price. Perhaps it's too much to say that one should memorize these pages, but certainly they establish very clearly the techniques which sales representatives should be aware of in endeavoring to command a superior price for their products and services.

All in all, the reader will have an exciting, but more importantly, profitable venture in reading this book. He or she will discover Larry's insights in such simple things as how one actually signals the customer that he or she can be beat up on price by using adverbs and adjectives in sentences where they talk price, to the profound suggestions on how to slam dunk sales when faced by stiff price resistance by the customer. In writing this book, Larry Steinmetz has made a quantum leap forward for those interested in selling at prices higher than their competitors in intensively competitive situations.

Roger Dawson, CSP
Author, YOU CAN GET ANYTHING YOU WANT
La Habra, California

PREFACE

This is the 10th book I've written. Everytime I write a book I wait until it's almost time for page proofs before I write the preface, the reason being I like to reflect on what the book really is about in order to say a few succinct statements about the book for the prospective reader.

I particularly like to write prefaces after the book is written because one gets perspective. The perspective I got for this preface came from a vacation I took just a week ago. I happened to read a piece of advertising literature of a small (albeit international) manufacturing company in one of the better known ski resort towns in Colorado. The first paragraph of that company's literature proudly boasts: "We are not just running a business, but living a lifestyle." I'm sure the people who are running that company are proud of that statement; genuinely believe that one need not be too serious about running their business -- that if you produce a good product, the product will sell itself and one need not worry about the vulgar details of operating a business in a business-like fashion. Another interesting part of this manufacturer's literature is that the enclosure with this literature compared this company's prices with competitors' prices and -- you guessed it -- this company's prices were lower than their competitors. That's right. They allegedly have a superior product and, furthermore, can sell it at a price lower than their competitors and (surely?) make money doing that.

Once you've read this book, you'll appreciate the sarcasm in the above paragraph. This book is about how you sell things at prices higher than your competitors, not how to give things away. The organization of this book essentially runs as follows. I start with the FACTS -- *and the facts are that most companies do go broke and business is a game of margins, not a game of volume.*

The second dimension of this book has to do with UNDERSTANDING. Selling at prices higher than your competitors requires an attitude and an understanding upon the part of the sales person. Some of that understanding includes the following: People (customers) don't buy on price alone. Furthermore, there are five bases on which one can compete in selling a product and price is only one of the five. Quality, service, sales capability, and ability to deliver the product to the customer, when they need it, where they want it, AND on time are the other factors. Each of those remaining four are far more significant than price. Another bit of understanding is that buyers really need and like a lot of things -- and low price isn't necessarily one of them. The sales rep who intends to sell at prices higher than their competitors needs to get inside the customer's head and understand how these customer needs and likes can fit into that sales rep's ability to command a higher price than competitors.

The third basic section of this book concerns REALITIES. Many business people, as well as many sales people, simply do not understand the economics of pricing. Most think they do; very few do. For example, have you ever asked a business person or a sales person how much additional volume of any product they have to sell to make up for a price cut? Usually you'll get some vague answer, or some wide range of answers like, "Twenty to forty percent more, I guess." And once in a while, you even get an honest answer such as, "Gee, I don't know." Business people are their own worst enemies, as are sales representatives. They tend to blindly believe that somehow, someway, if they get price competitive (i.e., cut the price) that they can make it up in volume. This section of the book, devoted to the realities of the marketplace, is absolutely essential for the business person to understand if he or she is to sell at prices higher than their competitors. As is developed in the text, it is precious difficult, if not impossible, to cut price and make it up in volume while, on the opposite end, it is often possible to raise price, lose volume, and make far more money. People who have attended the seminars that I do on HOW TO MAKE YOUR PRICES STICK and HOW TO SELL AT PRICES HIGHER THAN YOUR COMPETITORS have, over the years, related to me numerous testimonials concerning the fact that raising prices is not the end of the world. It does not cause sales to plummet, and oftentimes simply means that the company makes more money with less aggravation and heartache for those endeavoring to earn a living in that business.

The final, and major, portion of this book, has to do with WHAT TO DO ABOUT IT. The bulk of this book addresses such things as how to handle price pressure, price resistance and price competition. I spend a lot of time talking about how to face price-cutting by your competitors, as well as how to determine if it really is price that is the problem in the mind of the customer. I devote attention to understanding the very basics of the statement that your customer will tell you when your prices are too high - as well as tell you when your prices are too low. By analyzing those indicators of overpricing and underpricing which I develop, the sales reps can determine very accurately whether or not they should be able to realize a higher selling price in the marketplace.

Yet another very fundamental system of coping with price pressure in the marketplace is the material that I develop on tricks used by those serving in the roll of procurement officers in attempting to get the sales representative to cut his/her own price. From the feedback I've received from my seminar attendees, identifying these tricks have given sales people strong support in foiling the attempt of buyers to get sales people to cut their own price.

In this section of the book, I also discuss closing sales in the face of price resistance, as well as sales techniques to use in facing down price resistance. Finally, I even address the question of "Stoppers". Stoppers, of course, are the methods and techniques that sales reps use to stop customers from beating on them for additional price reductions.

All in all, I'm very pleased with the end result. I've been doing seminars on this subject for so many years I hate to think about when I started. But I do feel that in this book I have assembled a hard-nosed, let's-face-life-with-reality look at how those companies and individuals who make a lot of money selling at high prices manage to do so. They don't do it by cutting price. They do it by knowing the realities of selling at prices higher than one's competitors. They face facts, they understand customer buying motives, they face the realities of the economics of selling products and services and they know what to do about the customer who says, "Your prices are too high." I hope the reader will find this book every bit as productive as those who have heard me speak these words in public and private seminars -- and I wonder if that manufacturer in the mountains in Colorado will be in business next year when I make my next trip up there...

Lawrence L. Steinmetz, Ph.D.
Boulder, Colorado
January 1992

CHAPTER 1

MOST BUSINESSES FAIL
OR GO BROKE --
AND YOURS CAN, TOO

*"Our basic problem has been our
14 quarters of losses. And that's
because the price of the
equipment we build has been less
than the cost."*
Norman J. Ryker

Most businesses die. They start off, they expand a little bit, and then they die. Statistically, 16 out of 17 businesses that start in the United States will fail and/or go out-of-business -- most of them in the first two years of their existence. The average life expectation for all businesses in the United States is estimated at 7.5 years. One of the lines used to promote numerous business management seminars is: *If your business is not 8 years old, the odds are it never will be!* In fact, no less a business giant than Thomas J. Watson, the builder of IBM, in the first paragraph of his book, *A Business and Its Beliefs,*[1] wrote:

> "Of the top twenty-five industrial corporations in the United
> States in 1900, only two remain in that select company today.

---

1   Watson, Thomas J., *A Business and Its Beliefs: The Ideas That Helped Build IBM.*
(New York: McGraw-Hill) 1963, 107 pp.

> "One retains its original identity; the other is a merger of seven corporations on that original list. Two of those twenty-five failed. Three others merged and dropped behind. The remaining twelve have continued in business, but each has fallen substantially in its standing.
>
> "Figures like these help to remind us that corporations are expendable and that success, at best, is an impermanent achievement which can always slip out of hand."

Watson wrote the above in 1963!! Now, three decades later, the situation is, of course, far worse.

It is a matter of statistical fact that most businesses sooner or later fail. The statement that most businesses fail is just as true as if someone were to tell you that if you are not 80 years old, the odds are you never will be. The average life expectation for people in our society is just short of 80 years: for women it's just at 80 years; for men it's about 74-75. But on the average, we will all be dead and buried by the time we're 80. And, on the average, your business will be dead and gone before it is 8 years old.

SO MOST BUSINESSES FAIL. WHAT'S THAT GOT TO DO WITH MAKING YOUR PRICES STICK?

Most businesses do end up in bankruptcy court, being liquidated, or sold off because they aren't making any money. But why talk about failure? This book is about success -- about how to sell at a high price and how to make a profit for yourself and your company. Right? Well, one of the first things you need to recognize is that the fundamental problem in making your prices stick is that you're competing with people and businesses who are going broke. And when businesses start losing money, *THEY CUT THEIR PRICES.* In a desperate attempt to try to stay alive they slash their prices because they've always been told that they can make it up in volume. They think if they can just sell more then surely they will come out on top. But that doesn't work! When is the last time you've seen a business that had a going out of business price <u>increase</u>?

Most people have no idea how many businesses actually fail in the United States. Currently, it is estimated that there are just at 800,000 new businesses started in the United States each year, and there are only about 11,000,000 real businesses existing in the United States. Let's relate that number to another relevant figure. According to the U.S. Census Bureau, there are approximately 250,000,000 American people. That means that we roughly have one business for about every 23 people. Added to this is the fact that roughly only about 40% of our population work. Our work force, according to the U.S. Department of Labor, is just at 110,000,000 people. So now we roughly have one business for about every 10 employed people. Thus, if we have roughly 800,000 new businesses starting each year, and we have only 11,000,000 businesses, the failure rate has to be rather extensive or we're going to have more businesses than we have people to run them.

So maybe we should say that, *fortunately*, half of those 800,000 businesses that start will fail the first year. And that, *fortunately*, half of the remaining half will fail the second year. This means that roughly three out of four businesses that start will fail in the first two years of their existence. You need to keep this in mind when you come in from a hard day of selling, with your nose all bloodied, and your knuckles all skinned up, and you say to yourself, "We are getting killed; we are getting hammered; how can those guys sell at that price? If they can sell at that price, we can, too."

Well, friend, you have that part right. If *they* can sell at that price -- and go broke -- *you can too!* If you base your price on your competitor's price -- and he is going broke -- you will, too. Typically, someone among your competition is going broke, and is usually cutting prices on the way out. Owen Young, who is credited with having built General Electric, once said, "It's not the crook we fear in modern business; rather it's the honest guy who doesn't know what he is doing."

IT MAY BE ILLEGAL TO BE CROOKED, BUT IT ISN'T ILLEGAL TO BE STUPID

Who would you rather compete with, a crook or an idiot? If you think about it, you'll no doubt decide in favor of a crook. Have you ever seen a crook sell below cost? Have you ever heard anybody call the mafia *poor business people*? You may not approve of the mafia and their "business", but you have never heard anybody say they don't know how to make money!

Now let's talk about idiots. Have you ever seen an idiot sell below cost? Which idiot? And what day do you want to talk about? You see, Owen Young was right. Fundamentally, it is not the crook we fear in business, but rather it is the honest person. The people (or businesses) who don't know what they are doing are the ones who screw up the works. In essence, they are giving products and services away by cutting their price.

THE CAUSES OF BUSINESS FAILURE

Typically, when a business goes bust, especially if a business gets into enough trouble to have to file bankruptcy, three things occur:

1) They experience a period of declining gross margin;
2) Wages, as a percentage of sales, begin to increase; and
3) Sales volume begins to increase.

In this book, because we are dealing with the subject of how to make your prices stick, we are concerned about 2 of those 3 things: declining gross margin and increasing sales volume.

• DECLINING GROSS MARGIN.

Most businesses that go broke do so during a period of declining gross profit margin. Declining gross margin indicates *per se* that there is a pricing problem. For example, the way one calculates gross margin is by subtracting the cost of goods sold from sales.

Sales	$100	100%
COGS	$65	65%
GM	$35	35%

The only way that gross margin (as a percentage of sales) can go down is because the business either cut its price or failed to raise its price when its cost rose. For example, that can occur three different ways; but still, on net, it produces the same result -- the sales price is too low relative to the cost of goods sold. These three ways of doing the same thing, only different, is shown on page 6.

Declining gross margin inevitably signals a company that is experiencing a pricing problem which will result in trouble. It signals an inability to sell your products or services at a high enough price relative to your costs. Most companies that file for bankruptcy due to operational reasons have had a history of declining gross margin before they file. They often will blame it on "cost increases" but the net impact is declining gross margin because their selling price was too low relative to their cost.

• WAGES AS A PERCENTAGE OF SALES BEGIN TO INCREASE.

A second condition that normally prevails when a company fails is that, typically, wages as a percentage of sales begin to increase. This normally occurs because the company has too many people on the payroll. There are too many people sitting around on their hands, watching other people sitting around on their hands. But that's a subject that falls into another area of business management and not what we want to talk about here. But for the decision making executive, it is an area which must be watched because it is often difficult to cut down the work force even if they don't have anything to do. Don't let wages as a percentage of sales increase above that rate where you have good profitability, or your company will likely go broke -- even if it doesn't have a problem in making prices stick.

• SALES VOLUME INCREASES.

There's a third condition that normally prevails when a business goes bust. Most businesses that go broke do so during a period of sales volume increase. This statement shocks most people (especially those involved with sales) because most everyone thinks that a business fails as a result of a lack of sales volume. The facts are, however, that business is not a game of volume. *Business is a game of margins.* If a business doesn't maintain gross margin at an adequate level, it is going to go bust, *regardless* of its sales volume.

THE 3 WAYS GROSS MARGIN CAN DECLINE

A) If you *cut* price $5 to sell something, situation A transpires:

SITUATION A

Sales	$100	100%	$95	100%
COGS	$ 65	65%	$65	68%
GM	$ 35	35%	$30	32%

B) If you don't cut price, to get a sale, but *fail* to raise price when your costs go up $5, situation B transpires:

SITUATION B

Sales	$100	100%	$100	100%
COGS	$ 65	65%	$ 70	70%
GM	$ 35	35%	$ 30	30%

C) If you find your costs are going up $5 and raise your price only by the amount of your cost increase, situation C transpires:

SITUATION C

Sales	$100	100%	$105	100%
COGS	$65	65%	$ 70	67%
GM	$35	35%	$ 35	33%*

*Note: Your dollar gross margin stays at $35, but your gross margin as a percentage of your sales $ goes down from 35% to 33%. In short, raising your price the same dollar amount as your cost increase is a *de facto* price-cut as to your gross margin %. You must raise your selling price the same % as your % increase in costs if you are to maintain your gross margin % in the face of rising costs.

BUSINESS IS A GAME OF MARGINS, NOT VOLUME

Many large company leaders seem to blindly believe that volume and market share are the secrets to business success. If that is so, then why are there billion dollar corporations filing bankruptcy at the current rate of about 1 per month in the United States? As of the time of this writing, the world's largest retailer (Campeau) recently filed for bankruptcy; the world's second largest retailer (Sears) is in serious straits; the world's largest junk bond dealer (Drexel, Burnham, Lambert) is bankrupt; the United States' largest bus company (Greyhound) just filed for bankruptcy; the second largest convenience food chain (Circle K) is bankrupt; rumors abound that the largest convenience food chain (Southland) won't make it; and *USA Today* is anticipating the probable bankruptcy of the United States second largest airplane manufacturer (McDonnell). The people who had the Cabbage Patch Dolls as the hottest thing in the Christmas market a few years ago (Caleco) is bankrupt and such biggies as Eastern Airlines, Pan Am, Miniscribe, Integrated Resources, Resorts International, and M Corporation have recently bit the bullet and declared bankruptcy. Maxi Care and MacGregor Sporting Goods filed for bankruptcy on the same day -- March 16, 1989 -- "a vintage day for large company bankruptcies." Other giants (with big or biggest market share) have gone into bankruptcy or disappeared: Swift & Company (at one time the U.S.'s largest meat packer), Penn Central (at one time the U.S.'s largest public transportation company), and Railway Express Agency (one time the U.S.'s largest small package delivery company). Although most readers under the age of 30 have *never heard* of these last three companies, at one time each was perceived as invincible -- as was General Motors. "As goes General Motors, so goes the nation," was a famous expression of the 1960s. But as I write this, I read speculation from some very honored journals of business that General Motors may be bankrupt by the year 2020 or before.

The above examples should provide a fairly graphic picture that business is, indeed, not a game of volume and market share. A business must maintain an adequately high price against its costs (a high gross margin) or it is going to follow its well-known predecessors down the well-traveled path to bankruptcy court.

WE CAN MAKE IT UP IN VOLUME

When businesses get into financial difficulty, it's inevitably because some genius gets the bright idea that one can cut price and make it up in volume -- or at least be "competitive". Most people get that idea when they take a course in economics. In fact, if you have anything to do with selling or pricing, one of the worst things that may have happened to you is when you went to college and took Econ 101.

Just to emphasize the point that the bulk of our population think that the only way to do business is to cut price and make it up in volume, consider what happened as a result of airline deregulation. In 1978, President Jimmy Carter deregulated the airline industry. This meant that the airlines were then free to charge any price they wanted. How many airlines raised prices? Answer: None. How many kept the same prices? Answer: Virtually none. They all, in varying degrees, began to cut their prices. How many airlines have filed for bankruptcy since deregulation? Answer: As of the writing of this book, about 250. In fact, Senator Danforth, in the February 1990 issue of *Meeting News*[2] reported that of the 215 airlines created *after* deregulation, only 59 were still surviving in February 1990. Eleven years after deregulation began, roughly three of every four airlines that *started* between 1978 and 1990 had already failed. He was also quoted as saying that all of the low cost/price airlines had failed.

Man's ability to fail creatively is quite widely distributed in the population. The depths have not as yet been plumbed as to the new, novel and different ways somebody is going to figure out how to stink up a business. *But they all go back to one common behavioral pattern: they cut the price (to make it up in volume).* If you think you can match (or sell below) your competitor's prices, you need to understand that you will have an on-going, lifetime gun battle of survival which, sooner or later, you are going to lose. There is nothing that is ever going to make that go away.

---

2 "Washington Studies Impact of Airline Deregulation", *Meeting News,* February 1990, page 8.

SOME OF THE LARGER AIRLINES THAT HAVE
FILED FOR BANKRUPTCY SINCE DEREGULATION

Airline

Continental (twice)	Air One
Frontier	Pacific Express Airlines
Frontier Horizon	Wright Airlines
Air Florida	Capital Airlines
Air Illinois	Mid-Pacific Airlines
Pride Airlines	National Airlines
Braniff Airlines (three times)	People Express
Arrow Air	Eastern Airlines
Provincetown Boston Airlines	Presidential Airways
Britt Airlines	Pan Am
Northeastern Intl. Airlines	Midway Airlines
Air Atlanta	America West Airlines
Muse Airlines	Trans World Airlines

- ## WHY COMPANIES ALWAYS CUT PRICE WHEN THEY GET INTO TROUBLE.

Most everyone has heard the story of those industrious entrepreneurs who set out to make their fortune by buying watermelons for a buck each and selling them for $10 a dozen. That story has made the rounds for years. And, like any good joke, it is readily adaptable to anything. Just change the subject -- watermelons, exit signs, carpeting, hammers -- and make the local meat-head the butt of the joke. The way I originally heard it ran as follows: "See, there were these two guys from Texas who had a little money and this old pick-up truck. They heard they could buy these watermelons in Mexico for $1 each and they figured they could sell them for $10 per dozen. So, they went to Mexico, loaded the truck with watermelons and headed toward Dallas, selling off these watermelons at $10/dozen. They did a hell of a business and sold out of watermelons before they got half-way to Dallas. But, while sitting on the side of the road, counting their money, they noticed they were a little short of the amount they had started with. They wondered what the problem was since they had done such a brisk business and they finally figured it out. What they needed was a bigger truck."

Although you may have thought this was a new story the first time you heard it, there is documented proof that it has been around over 90 years. Paul Nathan[3], who wrote *How to Make Money in the Printing Businesss*, published the following in 1900:

> "If there is any one thing in the business management of a printing office that particularly commands the utter disapproval of successful printers as being worse than other evils that beset the trade, it is the cutting of prices. The method of getting work by lowering the price has absolutely nothing to recommend it, and it is contrary to common sense. The practice is absolutely wrong in principle, and the reasoning advanced in its support, stripped of its verbiage, is the equivalent of that of the old apple-woman who bought apples at a cent each and was selling them at ten cents a dozen, and when asked how she could make any money at that replied: 'By doing a very large business.' "

When a business gets into trouble it has a cash-flow problem and a margin problem -- not a profitability problem.   For example, let's consider the following:

> Question: Do the vendors to your company care whether:
>   (A) you're profitable or (B) you pay your bills?
> Answer: (B), pay your bills.

---

3   Nathan, Paul *How To Make Money In The Printing Business*, (New York: The   Lotus Press) 1900, p. 114.

Question: Do your employees care whether:
          (A) you're profitable or (B) you meet your payroll?
Answer: (B), meet payroll.

A business gets into trouble when it can't pay its bills and/or can't meet payroll. It has a cash-flow problem (or more correctly, a cash-trickle problem). This creates an intolerable situation for the company. If the bills aren't paid, the company will be cut-off from needed services and supplies; if payroll isn't met, there will be no one to do the work. So, the first thing the top brass starts worrying about is, "We've got to get some cash." How can the business get any cash? It has got to *sell* something! How to sell something? Use the old standby: *cut the price*. Unfortunately, cutting the price immediately creates the three danger signs which signal that the company may soon become a bankruptcy statistic: (1) gross margin goes down; (2) wages as a percentage of sales go up and (3) sales volume begins to increase.

A business's gross margin goes down when it cuts prices. But does the business cut wages when it cuts prices? No. So then wages as a percentage of sales go up -- and sales go up because of the lower prices. Those are the three conditions that *virtually always prevail* when a company really gets itself in trouble and ends up filing bankruptcy or having to sell-off or merge because it isn't making any money.

Many sales people have the feeling that when they're out in the marketplace, the only way to sell and compete is to cut their price when the competition starts cutting their price. They think, "Hey, man, we're getting killed. We're getting hammered. Our competitors are selling at a lower price than we are. They keep cutting our price. Well, if those guys can sell at that price, we can, too." So they come back to the head shed, to the boss, and they say, "Hey, boss, we're getting killed out there. If those guys can sell at that price, we can too." Well, the bottom line is -- *If those guys can sell at that price and go broke -- you can too.* Just because your competition is selling at a price or offering their product at a price lower than you are, doesn't mean you can -- or should even try to -- meet their price because most of that competition is going broke.

Maybe you *still* don't believe that most businesses go broke. Perhaps, you think it's only the little start-up companies that lose it -- not the big boys that "know

11

what they're doing". You think that big businesses don't go broke? Let me give you another example. *Inc.* [4] magazine, in May 1988, reported that, "We should not expect of our large corporations that they somehow possess a corporate fountain of youth. We should not mourn the fact that, in the 11 years between 1970 and 1981, 29% of the 1970 *Fortune 500* companies vanished as companies..." They go on to say that this, " 'vanishing rate' of a *Fortune 500* company is only two-and-a-half times less than the vanishing rate of a garage start-up today."

That not enough to suit you? Columbia University spokesman James A. Kennelley[5], Associate Director of Columbia Executive Program, in an effort to alert executives to look at what is going on in our business environment, states that, "Two of every five companies that appeared on the *Fortune 500* list in 1978 do not appear on the 1988 list!" Further, the Bankruptcy Data Source of Boston lists approximately 1100 public companies which have filed for Chapter 11 protection during the 1980s, approximately 110 per year. This list includes such giants ($100,000,000 or more in sales) as:

Penn-Dixie Industries; White Motor; Arctic Enterprises; Dynamic Instrument; First Mortgage Invest.; Frontier Airlines; FSC Corporation; Goldblatt Bros.; Itel Corporation; McLouth Street; Sambo's Restaurants; Seatrain Lines; AM International; Amarex, Inc.; Bobbie Brooks; Braniff International; Empire Oil & Gas; HRI Industries; KDT Industries; Manville Corporation; Nucorp Energy; Revere Copper & Brass; Saxon Industries; UNR Industries; Wickes; Anglo Energy; Baldwin United; Continental Airlines; Marion Corporation; Wilson Foods; Air Florida; Charter Company; Cook United; Crompton Company; MGF Oil; North American Car Corporation; Pizza Time Theatres; Storage Technology Corporation; Towner Petroleum; Transcontinental Energy; Becker Industries Corporation; Buttes Gas & Oil; Continental Steel Corporation; Dunes Hotels and Casinos; Evans Products; Nicklas Oil & Gas; A. H. Robins Company; Salant Corporation; Tacoma Boatbuilding; Wheeling-Pittsburgh Steel; American Adventure; CLC of America; Crutcher Resources; Crystal Oil Company; Global

---

4   *Inc.*, May 1988, p.21, Column 2.

5   Advertising piece, Columbia Executive Programs, Columbia University Graduate School of Business, New York, NY 10027, November 1988.

Marine, Inc.; LTV Corporation; McLean Industries; Mission Insurance Group; Oxoco, Inc.; Pettibone Corporation; Smith International, Inc.; Technical Equities Corporation; Texas American Oil Corporation; WedTech Corporation; Winn Enterprises; Allis-Chalmers Corporation; American Healthcare Management; Butterfield Equities, Inc.; Heck's, Inc.; Kaiser Steel Corporation; Michigan General Corporation; Phoenix Steel Corporation; Sharon Steel Corporation; Texaco, Inc.; Todd Shipyards Corporation; Western Real Estate Fund; Worlds of Wonder; Allegheny International, Inc.; American Carriers, Inc.; BASIX Corporation; Cardis Corporation; Care Enterprises, Inc.; Coleco Industries; Crowther McCall Pattern; De Laurentiis Enterprise Group; Financial Corporation of America; First RepublicBank Corporation; Public Service Co. of New Hampshire; Radice Corporation; Revco D.S., Inc.; Western Company of N.A.; American Continental Corporation; Bay Financial Corporation; Bicoastal Corporation; Braniff, Inc.; Brown Transport Co., Inc.; Continental Information Systems; Dart Drug Stores, Inc.; Eastern Air Lines; First Columbia Financial; First Farwest Corporation; Geothermal Resources; Hillsborough Holdings Corporation; Lomas Financial; Lone Star Technologies; Maxicare Health Plans; MCorp; Pantera's Corporation; Qintex Entertainment; Republic Health Corporation; Residential Res. Mortgage Investment; Resorts International; Rothschild Holdings, Inc.; Sahlen & Associates, Inc.; Southmark Corporation; Texas American Bancshares; Eagle-Picher; Pan Am; Bank of New England; Best Products Company; Hill; Carter Hawley Hale; Midway Airlines, America West Airlines and Trans World Airlines.

Still don't think most companies sooner or later fail? According to the *Standard Catalogue of American Cars*[6], there have been more than 5,000 companies and builders of automobiles in the United States. The American love affair with the automobile is well-known, yet most people can't accurately identify the fourth biggest, born-and-bred in the USA, manufacturer of automobiles that is still in business today and not under bankruptcy protection by the courts. Can you? It isn't American Motors Corporation (they had to be taken over by Chrysler); Checker quit building cars in 1982, and Avanti, Excalibur and Zimmer have all filed for bankruptcy. The top three are General Motors, Ford and Chrysler, but at the time of this writing I am not sure who

---

6   Kimes, Beverly Rae and Clark, Henry Austin, Jr., *Standard Catalog of American Cars, 1805-1942*, 2nd Edition, Krause Publications, Inc., 1989, 1568 pp.

holds fourth place -- or even if there *is* a fourth one. Yet, in the past 100 or so years, there have been nearly 5,000 automobile manufacturers come and go.

What we are talking about doesn't just involve an isolated segment of the business world. Failure occurs in all avenues -- big and small, established and start-up. But there is a commonality which exists -- most believe they can cut their price and make it up in volume, but they fail to consider what happens to their gross margin when they try to compete in this manner. As the quotation at the start of this chapter says, "The cause of our losses is that the *price* of the equipment we build *has been less than the cost.*"

CHAPTER 2

BUT COMPETITION KEEPS
CUTTING MY PRICE

*"No business opportunity is ever
lost. If you fumble it, your
competitor will find it."*
Business Quotes

Just because your competition is cutting their price doesn't mean that you can too and expect to survive. If your competitor has more money to lose than you do, *your* company will go broke first. The important thing to remember is that *your competition does not cut your price;* **you** *cut your price.* Your competitor may offer their product (or service) at a price lower than you offer yours, but you cut your price. Pogo the Possum said it all years ago when he said, "We have found the enemy and he is us." If anything occurs that causes your price to go down, it's a *self-inflicted* wound.

CUSTOMERS ONLY BUY ON PRICE -- OR DO THEY?

Unfortunately, many businesses and sales people operate under the false notion that people (and businesses) buy on price -- and price alone. Nothing could be further from the truth. Our research shows that price is virtually never the primary reason that anybody buys anything. In fact, if price were the only reason anybody bought anything, then only one guy -- the one with the lowest price -- would sell all there is to sell of that product. But that has never happened in the real world. So there must be some other reasons why customers buy from different sources.

There is also another bit of evidence that shows that customers don't buy on price. If price were the only reason anybody bought anything, WE WOULDN'T NEED SALES REPS! We wouldn't even need people to answer the phone and give a quote. A telephone computer could handle all our sales presentations on price, and a tape recorder could take all our orders. Of what earthly use would a sales rep be if customers bought only on price and aggressively searched for the best price? They would just call around to computers that answered phones and gave quotes, and then place their order at the sound of the tone.

WHO IS WEARING THE CHEAPEST SHIRT THEY COULD BUY?

Over and beyond the foregoing logic about people buying (or not buying) on price, let's do a simple test among ourselves. Right now, are you wearing the cheapest shirt (blouse, dress, etc.) you could buy? Now there may be a couple of you who will seriously believe that you are but, even so, let's explore this further. Would you have bought it if it didn't fit? What about the color and style? Well, then, what was more important? Price or fit, color and style? No doubt, you considered the price but what was the real deciding factor? Even if you still believe it was price -- at least you can see that price alone did not determine your decision. What about shoes? Would you buy the cheapest pair if they pinched your toes? And again, what about style and color? Would you have bought them if they were chartreuse? And had spots?

Some of you are going to say, "Yeah, but...!" " Yeah, but you are talking about consumer goods. I sell to businesses and industrial buyers. I deal with the trained bad actors that companies send to school to learn to buy on price." If you think businesses buy on price, next time you are around a group of senior management types, why don't you ask for a show of hands of all those in the group whose companies buy and use the cheapest machinery and equipment on the market. It would be very surprising if even one of them will raise a hand. People don't buy on price, and neither do businesses -- at least not very many of them. Many say they do; many even think they do. And most of your customers will tell you they do because *they are trying to get YOU to cut YOUR price.*

DO YOU BUY ON PRICE?

Many people do think they buy on price, and maybe you still think you do. So before we go any further, let's have a brief test: Consider the foregoing two paragraphs about price, price-buying, the shirt you are wearing, and the shoes you are wearing. Then take a moment and answer this question: Are you a price-buyer?

Yes_____   No_____

EREW OHW EM ROF DEKROW OHW SPER SELAS YNA NAC D'I .MEHT XIF RO -- MEHT NAC !SREYUB-ECIRP

You may have a little trouble reading the foregoing sub-head because it is printed on the page backwards. That is because I wanted you to honestly answer the question of whether or not you are a serious price-buyer. If you hold the foregoing subhead to a mirror, it will quit looking like Russian and will read as follows: I'D CAN ANY SALES REPS WHO WORKED FOR ME WHO WERE PRICE-BUYERS! *CAN* THEM -- OR *FIX* THEM.

There are two reasons for this statement, and they both hinge on the same fact: PRICE IS VIRTUALLY ALWAYS MORE IMPORTANT IN THE MIND OF THE SELLER THAN IN THE MIND OF THE BUYER. One experiment we conducted on customer buying motives involved 100 experienced purchasing agents/buyers and 100 inexperienced purchasing agents/buyers. They were asked how much of several products they would buy from various vendors. Almost every one of the inexperienced buying group picked the *same* vendor, who was, mathematically, the lowest priced. But *none* of the experienced buyers picked the lowest priced vendor. Rather, their vote was split between two other vendors at the rate of about 5 to 1. We asked those who picked the vendor most widely selected by the experienced buyers why they picked that vendor and they said *history of delivery.* We asked those experienced buyers who picked the other vendor and they said *quality standards of the vendor.*

The Typical Sales Rep's Idea of What They Teach in Purchasing and Buying Seminars

HOW TO BUY ON PRICE - A ONE DAY SEMINAR

A. Why You Want To Buy On Price.

B. Why You Don't Want To Pay Too Much.

C. Knowing Your Numbers -- A Practical Exercise on Accurately Identifying the Lowest Bid Price.

D. How Not To Be Confused About Quality -- That Stuff Is All The Same Anyhow.

E. Service -- Service -- Everybody Says Theirs Is The Best.
   - Why Service Is Unimportant.
   - Even If Their Service Is Better, There are Eight Good Reasons Not To Pay Extra To Get It.

F. All Sales Reps Are Liars -- You Must Only Consider Price.

G. Ascertaining The Lowest Number -- Basic Math Secrets You Can Use To Be Sure You're Committing To The Lowest Price.

H. So What If They Can Deliver It Yesterday When You Absolutely Have To Have It -- There Are Several Good Reasons To Buy From The Cheap Guy Anyway.

I. How To Beat Them Up On Price.

THE HOT STOVE PRINCIPLE

The foregoing reflects what is known as the "hot stove principle" which, loosely stated, says that if you have ever seen a cat jump on a hot stove, you'll probably never see the same cat jump on the stove again, even if it is cold. Once burned, you've probably learned your lesson. Customers and buyers learn lessons just like cats, and about as quick. What makes a purchasing agent awaken at 3:15 AM in a cold sweat thinking, "I'm going to get fired!"? It isn't that he/she paid too much for a product. What will get him/her fired is *THE CUPBOARD IS BARE!* "We don't have parts." "We don't have material." "We are out of supplies." "Where's that stuff I was supposed to get?" Those are the statements and questions that haunt PAs and buyers! Not: "How much did you pay?" That same PA or buyer who tells the sales rep that "Parts is parts" knows damn well that parts aren't parts when they *don't have any parts!* Terror is the only emotion in the buyer's mind when the big boss says, "Where are those...(parts) (supplies) (materials) (etc.)? Now I have to shut this job down...Send a crew of people home...Can't fill this order...Can't complete this job."

If there is any doubt that price is not as important as delivery or quality, and perhaps even service, here is a simple experiment which can be conducted in your own company. First thing tomorrow, go to your bookkeeper (or whoever writes checks in your company) and ask for a 100% accurate list of vendors that your company *paid* during the last two years. Having done that, you now have a list of all the vendors who actually got a sale to your company -- i.e., you ordered, they shipped, you paid. Nothing less constitutes a sale (a sale is not consummated until the check has cleared the bank). Now, with that 100% accurate list of your vendors, go to your purchasing people and point out to them the vendors you bought from a year ago, but didn't use last year; and the vendors you used last year to supply to your company those products you had bought from the other vendors a year before. Ask them WHY they quit using those vendors, and what was most important on their mind when they picked the vendors they used to replace the ones they dropped.

In a study of 64 firms, we discovered that *PRICE* was the reason for dropping a particular vendor only 8.1% of the time. That in 70.2% of the cases, a *DELIVERY* problem was the trigger event that caused one vendor to be dropped and another one used to replace them [7].   This makes the following four points:

1. A delivery problem is virtually always the trigger event that causes loss of a sale to an existing customer.

2. Your customer does not care *why* you stunk-up delivery. He only knows two things: (A) it isn't there and (B) it is *your* fault

3. Your customer does not care *how good* your reason was for stinking-up delivery. *He doesn't even care if your reason is true!*   Even if you have pictures of the fire, flood, hurricane, tornado, volcanic eruption, earthquake, etc., he still only knows two things: (A) it isn't there and (B) it's your fault.

4. You stink-up delivery *one time* and your customer will find another vendor -- *because he has to.* He wouldn't have ordered your product if he didn't want and/or need it -- and he needed it on time.

MOST SALES REPS THINK PRICE IS
MORE IMPORTANT THAN IT IS

It is not unusual to find sales reps who think price is more important than other factors when it comes to a customer making a purchase decision. The research referred to above indicates that price is more important in the mind of the seller than in the mind of the buyer. This brings us back to the two reasons that make a price-buyer a poor prospect as a sales rep (and why I say I'd can any sales rep who worked for me who was a price-buyer). They are:

• PRICE-BUYING SALES REPS PROJECT THEIR FEELINGS TO THEIR CUSTOMERS.

Projection, of course, is the word the pychologists use to communicate the idea that people project (or impute) their ideas, feelings and emotions to others. The same as a sales rep says, "I'm just like anybody else, I put my pants on just like anybody else," he/she also says, "I'm just like anybody else. I buy on price.

---

7   The complete breakdown was as follows: 70.2% dropped a vendor because of delivery problems, 9.4% because of quality problems, 8.1% because of price, 6.2% because of service (mostly poor) and 6.1% because the vendor went out of business -- another form of delivery problem.

Therefore, I know my customer buys on price." But that is faulty logic. Just because you buy on price doesn't mean that your customer buys on price, anymore than just because you are a good driver means your customer is a good driver or that just because you put your pants on, left leg first, while sitting down, means that your customer does the same thing. Maybe they put their pants on right leg first, standing up. The same as I can easily think of four different ways people put their pants on, I can think of at least four different motives that people have to buy something. Price is only one of them.

Projection means, in essence, it takes one to call one. It takes a price-buyer to call a price-buyer, and studies show clearly that price-buyers "see" (at least they think they "see") a lot of price-buyers. But that is because all buyers look like price-buyers to a price-buyer.

• PRICE-BUYING SALES REPS TELL THE CUSTOMER THEY THINK THEIR PRICES ARE TOO HIGH AND INVITE THEIR CUSTOMERS TO BEAT THEM UP ON PRICE.

It is literally true that sales reps who think their prices are too high and "know", in their heart, gut and brain that the customer can "get it cheaper down the street" will indicate this to their customers. They do this as much by things they don't say and do, as by things they do. And the number one thing they *don't* do that invites the customer to beat them up on price is: they *don't* talk price.

WHAT HAPPENS WHEN YOU DON'T TALK PRICE

In one study conducted a few years ago, it was found that up to 94% of sales people, when making a sales call, will not talk price *until* the customer asks about the price. Further, 44% of the sales reps, when asked the price, would change the subject, and about one-third would never say the price, preferring to write it down or point at it.

Do you have any idea what not talking price says to your customer? It says you are scared. After all, if your price was such a good deal, you'd be willing to talk about it, wouldn't you? And for those who write it down, or point at it -- "Here, you can see our price is...", are you afraid of your voice cracking or that you'll sound nervous if you say your price? Sales reps who are nervous about their price virtually always signal the customer that they are nervous (and think their price is too high) by the way they (don't) handle price. Coughing, choking, stuttering, stammering, pointing at the price, changing the subject, avoiding the issue -- all of these clearly signal the customer that you are not comfortable with your price. Until you can credibly, comfortably and confidently tell your customer, "This is the price. I sell a lot of it at this price, and I fully expect your order at this price," I can guarantee your customer will beat you up on your price. There is an acid test to use here to determine if you can credibly handle price. You must be able to handle price like you handle the time of day:

Q: "What time is it?"
A: "It is 3:15."
Q: "What is your price on this?"
A: "The price is $200."

Further, avoiding the statement of the price, or lack of credibility in handling the price, isn't the only thing that signals to your customer that you are negotiable. One of the other ways you clearly invite your customer to beat you up on price is to use adverbs and adjectives when you talk price.

- ## USING ADVERBS AND ADJECTIVES WHEN YOU TALK PRICE.

Adverbs and adjectives are a flag to the customer that your price is negotiable. Consider, for example, the implication of the statement "Our *usual* price is $200," and the statement, "Our price is $200." Adverbs and adjectives limit, modify or specify things about the noun, pronoun, verb, adjective or adverb with which they are used. Therefore, they clearly imply that *there is more than one kind* of noun, pronoun, verb, adverb or adjective. When you say, "Our usual price is...", you clearly make the customer think that you have more than one price -- i.e., you are negotiable. Try substituting any of the following adverbs or adjectives for the word "usual" in the above sentence, and see what you get -- or use your own special adverb or adjective:

Regular	Lowest
Normal	Best
List	Reduced
Book	Basic

Adverbial and adjectivial phrases are also used like adverbs and adjectives, but they are used to "cushion the blow" of giving the price to the customer. These always signal the customer that the sales rep's price is negotiable or that the sales rep feels his/her price is too high. These "cushioning techniques" take on a variety of forms, such as:

- Those that clearly show that the sales rep is afraid that his/her price is too high:

    "You better sit down before I give you my price."

    "You better buckle your seat belt before I lay this price on you."

    "Isn't it a crime, the price they charge for this stuff these days?"

    "The best I can do is..."

- Those that flatly state that the sales rep's price is negotiable:

    "You know I want to work with you on this."

    "You know we've valued having you as a customer over these many years."

    "I've been selling to you for a long time, Mr. Customer, and I sure don't want to lose your account."

    "I can let you have it for only $200, if..."

    "Since you are one of our larger customers, maybe we can work with you a little on this price."

- Those that invite or challenge the customer to look around or do comparison pricing. These include jewels such as:

    "Our price is lower than anybody's."

    "Comparatively speaking, I think we have the best price in town."

    "By buying from us, you can use these for as little as 23¢ each time you use it in a normal year."

    "Our new, reduced price is..."

    "Why, in the overall picture, using our product will hardly cost you anything."

    "Our price is scarcely more than you'd pay for a soft drink at the ball game."

- Those that clearly state: **BEAT ME UP.** Examples include:

    "Tell me where I need to be."

"What do I have to do to get your business?"

"Am I in the ballpark?"

"How's 27¢ sound to you?"

"Would you be willing to pay $40 for this?"

"Could you pay $40 for this?"

"Of course, I can give you an even better price, if..."

"You do intend to buy a lot from us this year, don't you? If you think you might order more than X amount this year, I might be able to work a better price for you."

"Of course, you know these cost more if you only buy two at a time. But if you bought three, I could maybe knock off another 50%."

"Well, we look at each order separately."

"Is $15 O.K.?"

"You know, we're giving you one heck of a deal here."

Eye movement also alerts the customer that you can be beat-up on price. Your eyes inevitably tell on your sincerity -- unless, perhaps, you are an Oscar-winning actor or actress. When you say a price you don't really believe, you'll almost always break-off eye contact and look down. Check out eye movement research at your local library, if you wish to read more about this.

Other factors which signal to customers that the sales rep is negotiable include such things as:

- The sales rep is overly eager to book the order.
- The sales rep volunteers that they can give quantity discounts.
- The sales rep stresses non-price issues and avoids talking price.
- The sales rep "WOWS" -- i.e., indicates that this is an exceptionally large order.
- A standard price quote is made.
- The sales rep initiates options that would lower the overall price.

CHAPTER 3

DETERMINING YOUR COMPETITIVE EDGE

"We have found the enemy, and he is us."
Pogo

You sell any kind of product or service on the basis of competitive edge. Your competitive edge fundamentally boils down to five things: (1) Price, (2) Quality, (3) Service, (4) Advertising/Promotion/Salesmanship, and (5) Delivery. We will talk about price, quality, advertising, promotion and salesmanship in this chapter, salesmanship and service in Chapter 4, and non-salesmanship (why and when and who not to sell to) and delivery in Chapter 5.

PRICE

One part of your competitive edge may be price. It is true that some people (businesses) do buy products and services seemingly on price. And I know that many readers face customers who say the only important thing is price. But our research shows that price is virtually *never* the primary reason someone buys something. It is seldom even the secondary reason. Usually it's a third consideration at best. Many readers will say, "If you don't think people buy on price, why don't you follow me around on some sales calls. Why just yesterday I had a prospective customer say to me that there's only three things important when he buys: 'The first one is price, the second one is price and the third one is price.'"

I know your customers will tell you that. They'll tell you that because they are trying to get *you* to cut *your* price. But their behavior belies their words. In fact, many people get very nervous even thinking about buying something that is low priced. Indeed, there are probably more people who will buy products or services on the basis of the price being HIGH as there are those who will buy on the basis of the price being low. You've probably even heard people contemplating making a purchase who say, "The only thing that really worries me about this deal is that the price is so low."

If you don't think people buy on *high price*, let's consider another example. Will you go out to the low price bidder for your brain surgery? Probably not. Because fundamentally, deep down, you really feel that you "get what you pay for" and the thought of going to the low price bidder for your brain surgery messes your mind. Most of us have an intrinsic feeling that price has something to do with the *quality* and the *value* of the product, or the service, that we are buying. In fact, most of us feel that price makes a statement about not only the quality of the product or service, but even to some degree, about the advisability of doing business with a low price seller.

PRICE MAKES A STATEMENT - A CREDIBILITY STATEMENT

If I told you I had a brand new Rolls Royce parked out front that I'd let you have for $47,000, the first thing you'd ask me is, "What's wrong with it?" And the second thing you'd ask is, "Do you have title to it?" Because you could not believe that I would offer to sell you a new Rolls Royce for $47,000 unless something was wrong with it, or it was stolen. Price makes a statement not only about the quality of what you are selling, but also the very advisability of even buying it. If your price is too low, the customer thinks there may be something wrong with it.

Now, let's look at the flip side. If I told you I had a new Rolls Royce I'd sell you for $300,000, what would you say? You'd probably say something like, "Really? What makes that car worth $300,000? I want to see that." TRANSLATION: "Tell me, show me, *sell* me on why I, or anyone, would pay you $300,000 for that or any car."

Price makes a statement; a credible statement. Just as people will believe you when you tell them you are cheaper (and they will believe that in every sense of the word -- in your price, your quality and your value), they will also believe you when you say you are higher priced (again in every way -- price, quality and value). Sales people who sell at high prices know that you use a high price to make a credibility statement about your product being better -- i.e, if it costs more, it probably is worth more. And they know that by acknowledging that your price is higher than your competitor's prices, you trigger a "the hell you say" response in your customers which creates the most *receptive, responsive* atmosphere in which to sell your product.

QUALITY

Low price is only one area of what you can compete on. It's also the absolute dumbest thing that you can compete on. If you want to earn some money as a sales rep, you'd better learn to compete on something other than low price; and one aspect of selling that is extremely important to the customer is quality. How important, as a competitive edge, is quality of the product (or service)? It's very important. In some cases it can be the single, most important reason a customer buys.

BICYCLE HELMETS FOR SALE

Good Quality   **Better Quality**   **Best Quality**

Special $10   Deluxe $40   **Guaranteed Protection**
Meets all mandatory and recommended standards of all testing agencies
$120

If you have a $10 head, buy a $10 helmet!!!

- SELLING QUALITY.

Selling quality is easy -- *if you have it and you know what it is*. Fortunately everybody has quality. Unfortunately, not everyone knows what quality means -- and consequently they have a tough time selling quality.

Most sales reps will tell you that quality means best. *Quality does not mean best.* Quality means conformance to standards and expectations -- to your customer's standards and expectations. Quality means the *right* stuff; not the best stuff. Quality is the *correct* stuff for your customer's requirements and needs, not the best stuff made.

The word *quality* and the word *best* are not synonyms. For example, what is a quality tire for your car? The only way to answer that question is to ask a question: What are you going to use the car for? Are you talking about an Indy 500 tire? Or are you talking about a racing slick? Perhaps you are talking about a studded snow tire. You buy the best racing slicks you can get, put them on your power-traction wheels, and see how fast you can accelerate in 6" of snow. Or put racing slicks on your front wheels and see how fast you can stop on wet pavement, going downhill. You might say that you bought "the best tires I could buy", but I'm afraid you'll be disappointed in their performance under those conditions.

Quality does not mean best. If quality means best, then why do we always have to define quality? Why does the mail-order catalogue say this is our "good quality" baseball glove, this is our "better quality" baseball glove and this is our "best quality" glove? The catalogue could just as easily say things like, this is our "good quality" glove, this is our "lesser quality glove" and this is "the most rotten quality glove ever stitched together". But they are all *quality* gloves.

- QUALITY CAN BE THE WRONG STUFF.

Many sales people can't make their prices stick because they try to sell either too high quality or inferior quality for the needs of the customers. If you want to sell quality, you better have "the right stuff". If you don't have the right stuff for your customer, you have a problem. You are a fool as a sales rep to try to jam the wrong stuff down your customer's throat. Selling certainly includes telling your customers that your stuff is the correct stuff (and why it is the correct stuff) for

28

them. But if your stuff is not the right stuff -- if you are selling high quality walnut wood and your customer only needs cheap plywood -- the only way you'll get your customer to buy the wrong stuff is to cut your price. If I'm building fine furniture, I might buy your walnut -- but if I'm putting in sub-flooring, I won't: I don't need it, don't want it and can't afford it. And the only way you'll sell me high quality walnut for sub-flooring is to cut your price.

BUT I SELL A COMMODITY - AND YOU HAVE TO SELL A COMMODITY ON PRICE

Let me make another strong statement about sales reps. Not only would I can any sales rep who works for me who is a price-buyer; I'd can any sales rep who works for me who views my product as a commodity. Let me explain why I say that.

Many sales people feel that they are in a commodity business and they believe, because of that, they must sell on price. Nothing is further from the truth. Just because one is selling a commodity doesn't mean that one must sell on price. A commodity, by definition, is any item about which there are no discernible differences, one from another. For example, suppose I have two water glasses for sale which are identical. If I tell you one is for sale for two pennies and one is for sale for one penny (and you are buying water glasses) which one are you going to buy? You are going to buy the one penny glass. Other things being equal, people buy on price. Right?

Many people believe that, other things equal, customers buy on price. But the facts are, even that is not true. First off, other things are seldom, if ever, equal. Secondly, and more importantly, *it is the sales rep's job* to make sure the customer knows (A) that other things are *not* equal and (B) that the customer knows why he/she should buy the sales rep's (higher priced) commodity item. A sales rep must differentiate his/her company's product and services from the competitor's somehow, some way. That is what selling is all about. Otherwise, a computer could answer our phone, give the customer a price quotation and a tape recorder could "write up" the order.

Furthermore, there is ample evidence that even when the product is equal -- identical -- people don't always buy on price. For example, if I were to offer to sell you a gallon of gasoline for $1.00 or an identical gallon -- and I mean *identical* gallon -- for $1.05, would you pay me the $1.05 or the $1.00? You will probably say that you'd only pay the $1.00. But the truth is many, many people will pay the $1.05 -- as is evidenced by the *billions* of gallons of gasoline sold in the United States when people purchase gasoline *using their credit cards instead of cash.* At many service stations in the United States, when one punches "credit" instead of "cash" one has voluntarily elected to pay about a 5% premium for the *identical* gasoline -- not just *almost* identical -- *THE IDENTICAL* -- gasoline. And consider what one pays for the same gasoline if the attendant pumps the gas for them. Furthermore, consider what one voluntarily pays for gasoline when one turns in a rental car and hasn't topped off the tank -- 50% to 80% more. But that's different -- the company is paying for it and we all know that companies, if not individuals, *always* buy on price.

The facts are, other things are never equal -- and even if the product is identical, customers don't necessarily buy on price. They say they do because they are trying to get *you* to cut your price. But their behavior belies the truth of what they say! The point is, even if one is selling a commodity -- a genuine commodity -- people still don't buy on price. Household consumers don't and businesses don't either.

While we are on the subject of commodities, incidentally, one should understand that most "commodities" are not commodities. For example, coal isn't coal, oil isn't oil, grain isn't grain, peanuts aren't peanuts and cement isn't cement. If you believe cement's cement, why don't you go back to Skokie, Illinois to the Portland Cement Association, stand around and say "cement's cement". I guarantee it won't be long before they are going to ask you: "What kind of cement are you talking about?" There are different kinds of cement, even though most people who buy cement will tell the cement salesman "Cement is cement." And even when one is talking about the *same kind* of cement, any given manufacturer of cement can differentiate their product from a competitor's by putting their brand on their product. In essence, this says that this is cement like the other guy's; but we made it and by buying *ours*, you are getting *our* quality control, *our* service, *our* delivery, *our* company's policies and procedures, *our* way of doing things, *our* billing procedures, *our* order turnaround, *our* friendly service, *our* care and attention, *our* ease of doing business with, etc., etc.

YEAH, BUT YOU ARE BUYING IT FROM US

Wholesalers and distributors are, of necessity, often selling the same stuff. Let's say you are a soft drink distributor and you carry Coca Cola, 7-Up and Pepsi products. Your competitor, another distributor, also carrys Coca Cola, 7-Up and Pepsi products. Now Coke's Coke. And 7-Up's 7-Up. Right? All Coca Colas are made to the same formula, and all 7-Ups are, likewise, the same. Therefore, if you are going to sell Classic Coke against your competition, who also sells Classic Coke, then you've got to sell on price, don't you?

NO! You don't have to sell on price. You can sell on several things *other than* price. This includes not only being easier, better and more convenient to do business with, but also advertising/promotion and salesmanship.

How important is advertising, promotion and salesmanship in selling? Well, if the customer doesn't know about it, you're not going to do any good selling it. Years ago, an exceptionally successful business woman who started an incredibly successful business, gave me this little rhyme:

> *He who has a thing to sell*
> *and goes and whispers in a well*
> *is not so apt to get the dollars*
> *as he who climbs a tree and hollers.*

DO YOU APPROVE OF SELLING?

How significant is capability and willingness to *sell?* My experience is that it often makes all the difference in getting a sale. *Many sales reps really don't like selling.* In fact, a lot of sales people think selling is just a notch above ambulance chasing. The truth is, more than 40 percent of the sales reps I've tested *fundamentally don't approve of selling* -- and my educated guess is that about 90 percent of our total population doesn't approve of selling.

ORDER FORM

HORIZON PUBLICATIONS, INC.
3333 IRIS AVENUE
BOULDER, COLORADO 80301
(303) 442-8114 (800) 323-2835
FAX (303) 442-2803

PLEASE SEND ME THE FOLLOWING BOOKS AND
TAPES BY LAWRENCE L. STEINMETZ, PH.D.:

BOOKS	QTY		AMOUNT
NICE GUYS FINISH LAST (2 lbs)	_____	@ $24.95 each	_____
HOW TO SELL AT PRICES HIGHER THAN YOUR COMPETITORS (2 lbs)	_____	@ $24.95 each	_____
JENNY THE PENNY by Kelly Fano (1 lb)	_____	@ $9.95 each	_____

AUDIO TAPES	QTY		AMOUNT
MANAGING THE UNSATISFACTORY PERFORMER (6 lbs)	_____	@ $85.00 each	_____
FIRST LINE MANAGEMENT (6 lbs)	_____	@ $100.00 each	_____
MANAGING A FAST GROWING RETAIL BUSINESS (6 lbs)	_____	@ $70.00 each	_____
MANAGING A FAST GROWING MANUFACTURING COMPANY (6 lbs)	_____	@ $75.00 each	_____
HOW TO MAKE YOUR PRICES STICK (6 lbs)	_____	@ $115.00 each	_____
HOW TO SELL AT PRICES HIGHER THAN YOUR COMPETITORS (6 lbs)	_____	@ $115.00 each	_____

VIDEO TAPES	QTY		AMOUNT
HOW TO MAKE YOUR PRICES STICK PACKAGE (10 lbs)	_____	@ $800.00 each	_____
HOW TO MAKE YOUR PRICES STICK PREVIEW (includes postage)	_____	@ $15.00 each	_____
HOW TO SELL AT PRICES HIGHER THAN YOUR COMPETITORS PKG. (10 lbs)	_____	@ $800.00 each	_____
HOW TO SELL AT PRICES HIGHER THAN... PREVIEW (includes postage)	_____	@ $15.00 each	_____

* Continental U.S. postage based on
weight per item indicated in (lbs) after
each item.

Up to 3#	$ 4.50
4# to 9#	$ 6.75
10# to 15#	$ 9.50
over 15#	please call

(example: 2 books @ 2 lbs each = 4 lbs)

** Colorado residents only.

Sub Total _____

Postage & handling* _____

Sales Tax 6.91%** _____

TOTAL _____

PRICES SUBJECT TO CHANGE
ALL SALES FINAL

☐ Check Enclosed

Charge To:
☐ American Express
☐ Master Card
☐ Visa

Send To _____

Company Name _____

Street Address _____

City _____ State _____ Zip _____

Phone Number _____

Card Number _____ Exp. Date _____

Name on Card _____

Signature _____

Sales reps *sell* things. In contrast to what? Mechanics. Mechanic is the word that I use to describe the sales rep who figures the product ought to be so good *it will sell itself.* The mechanic is the sales rep who believes in the better mousetrap theory.

Most sales reps say they are peddlers -- but many are not. For example, how do you feel about the advertising on the preceeding page in this book for the audio and video tapes for sale on the subject of how to make your prices stick? Would you say this is crass commercialism -- or a good business practice which apprises the reader of a product that is available to help them learn how to sell at a high price -- product that, perhaps, they didn't know was available in the market place? Or how do you feel about the person who calls you at 6:30 in the evening when you're having your dinner and tries to sell you light bulbs? There ought to be a law against that, right?[8]

If you think telemarketing is just interrupting someone's dinner to try to peddle light bulbs, you're definitely not sales rep material. Some of the greatest marketing success stories I can tell you are about people who have gone into telemarketing to appraise prospective customers of products that the customers wanted/needed and did not know were available. Telemarketing can be a real service to your customers. While many people may consider the dinner time phone call as intolerably inconsiderate of their privacy, there are many home-bound individuals, who have limited access to shopping, that welcome this type of service.

Most people have a certain degree of antipathy towards selling, especially when done aggressively -- and salespeople do, too. A lot of sales people think the old "shucks, golly, gee whiz, I don't imagine you'd want to buy this" approach to selling is too strong -- let alone telling a customer that he needs, wants and can afford your product and ought to buy it.

---

8   For evidence that many people think -- literally -- that there ought to be a law against telemarketing, see *USA Today*, Tuesday, June 11, 1991, p. 1B. There it explains that there are such laws already in existence in 28 states, and that there are very strong efforts currently being made to further legally control telemarketing throughout the United States. They also point out the fact that 28% of the telephone numbers are **unlisted** primarily because the telephone subscriber does not want to receive sales calls -- and is willing to pay a premium for this **unlisted** service to avoid such calls.

33

How To Sell At Prices Higher Than Your Competitors

Most people have heard of H. Ross Perot. He's the guy who built Electronic Data Systems (EDS) years ago. That was before he ran for President of the United States. *Forbes*[9] magazine says that he's worth about $2,400,000,000. -- and he made all that money in about 30 years. Do you know how much money that is? If he has that money invested at 10% interest, his interest income is about $650,000 PER DAY!! I'm not saying everybody can sell like an H. Ross Perot. But I think sales people can learn a lot from a man like Perot. There is an article about him in *Business Week*,[10] which says something about his selling skills:

> "Perot's initial challenge was to rise above his own success. He joined IBM in Dallas in 1956 after graduating from Annapolis and finishing his tour of duty. Though he was ignorant of computers -- he thought the company just made typewriters -- Perot quickly became a problem. He was so good at selling computers that his superiors didn't know what to do with him. He was already making so much money as a salesman that a promotion would have meant a pay cut. Perot, wanting action, said he wouldn't mind taking a pay cut to be promoted or even a smaller sales fee if IBM would turn him loose. IBM obliged, slashing his commission by 80% and raising his quota. Perot filled his 1962 sales quota on January 19th. "

Nineteen days to fill his new, higher quota -- and one of those was New Year's Day, and another four of those days were weekend days. Truth is, he really only had 14 working days to fill his new, higher quota.

Forget about Perot the politician. Think about Perot the salesman. Not everybody can be as great a salesman as H. Ross Perot, but most can do a lot better than they do. The first way to improve is to learn that there is a lot more to selling than price. Even if you're selling a commodity, and even if your competitor's quality is identical to yours, you still don't need to sell on price. Maybe your competitive edge is advertising, promotion or, as was in Perot's case, salesmanship. Or maybe it is something known as service.

---

9   *Forbes*, Volume 152, No. 9, October 18, 1993, p. 121.

10   *Business Week*, October 6, 1986, p. 62.

CHAPTER 4

SERVICE AS YOUR
COMPETITIVE
EDGE

"Anyone who thinks the customer
isn't important should try
doing without him for a period of
ninety days"
Business Quotes

How important is service in selling a product or service? It, too, can be *the* thing that makes or breaks your sale. It may be the only reason anybody buys anything. Service is incredibly important. And the good news is: it is incredibly *easy* to compete on service because very few businesses *want* to compete on service -- real service. *Most businesses are run by the people that work in that business and most of those people run that business for themselves.* They often treat the customer as a schmuck.

• WE ARE YOUR FULL-SERVICE BANK -- WE ARE OPEN
    FROM 10:00 TO 3:00.

Businesses often give minimal service to their customers, but they tell themselves that they give a lot. Your friendly, full-service bank is probably a good case in point. If your bank is so full of desire to give you good service, how come they are only open to lend you money from 10:00 to 3:00 -- except holidays and weekends when they are closed -- and will only lend you money if you don't need it? Why aren't they open from 3:00 to 10:00, and all day Saturday? I'll tell you why -- because the bank's management and employees don't want to be open then. Your banker's basic idea is: You can't be playing golf by 4:00 p.m. unless you close by 3:00 p.m.

And how about this line (if you believe people whose job it is to give you service want to serve you): "I'm from the government and I am here to *help* you."   And they say that with a straight face. Much like the professor who says, "The University is really a nice place when the students are gone," or the stewardess who says, "Isn't it nice on this flight; we hardly have any passengers." And then there's the customer service rep who takes the phone off the hook so he can "get his job done" or the desk clerk who says, "If that phone would only quit ringing, I could make some headway." The list could go on and on -- but you get the idea. You seldom hear anyone say, "This was a great day at the office. I was so busy I didn't have time for lunch."

SELLING SERVICE INSTEAD OF PRICE -- OR EVEN QUALITY

One of the big success stories in business and selling are the achievements of Tom Monaghan. Tom Monaghan is the guy who built Domino's Pizza. *Forbes*[11] magazine estimates his worth as at least $450 million. And how did he do that? His success came from selling service -- *charging for pizza, but selling service.* The key to his sales success was his sales slogan: "Domino's (Pizza) Delivers." Is it the best pizza in town? Very few will argue that it is the best. Is it the lowest priced pizza in town? Hardly -- usually not even close. It is more apt to be among the highest priced. Is he the most effective salesman in town? Very few will even argue that, although he gets the word out that he will do what he says he will. Maybe it's because he has no competition. Wrong again -- seems like he has a competitor on every corner. Then what is his secret to success? He delivers pizza - on time - like he said he would.

---

11 *Forbes*, Volume 152, No. 9, October 18, 1993, p. 222.

How many pizza shops are willing to *deliver* pizza, and how many rely on the fact that they cook "the best pizza in town" to sell their product? By our count in a few selected cities, less than 28% of the pizza shops in the U.S. deliver pizza. Most think that if they *cook* good pizza, the customer will beat a path to their door. Their mentality is: If you want some good pizza, *come to me* and I'll cook it for you. But don't expect me to deliver it. We aren't starting that nonsense. We do that, and the next thing you know, you'll want it *hot* when we get it there.

At a recent seminar, an attendee who was in the refrigerator and freezer supply business for hotels and restaurants in the Miami area said that in the metropolitan Miami area there are about 1,100 new restaurants opened each season. But, he also said that the total number of restaurants in Miami has not changed significantly in the past 10 years. This means that about 1,100 restaurants *fail* in Miami each year.

It is no secret that one of the industries in the United States with an incredibly high failure rate is the restaurant business. And the reason for this is that most people who operate restaurants are mechanics who run their business *for themselves* and treat the customer like a necessary evil. For example, if you have ever talked to someone who has failed in the restaurant business, you often find that their thinking before they opened their restaurant, went something like this:

> "I'm going to open a restaurant, cook good food, serve generous portions, and charge fair prices. No-no, I'm not going to do any advertising. No, I'm only going to do word-of-mouth advertising, for I know if I cook good food, serve generous portions, and charge fair prices, the world will beat a path to my door."

Wrong. You can't go into the restaurant business and succeed because you want to cook good food. You have to want to *sell* the food that has been cooked whether it is good or not. Not all successful restaurants have the best food around, but most that are successful know how to *sell.* If you don't know how to sell your product, I don't care how good your product is, you likely will find your business another statistic in the failed business column.

THE BETTER MOUSETRAP THEORY

If a man can write a better book, preach a better sermon, or make a better moustrap than his neighbor, though he builds his house in the woods, the world will make a beaten path to his door.

Ralph Waldo Emerson

You can have an unbelievably good product, but if you don't know how to sell it, you won't make any money. If you believe in the theory that "He who has a better mousetrap will find the world will beat a path to his door," you have no business in business. Ralph Waldo Emerson is credited with making this statement, which is interesting because he certainly was not a successful business person. In fact, Ralph Waldo Emerson apparently had a fair degree of contempt for business people and sales types in particular. By profession, Ralph Waldo Emerson was an ordained minister. Now, there is certainly nothing wrong with being an ordained minister, but Ralph Waldo Emerson was a doubly poor, ordained minister. First, he apparently wasn't very good at it; and second, because of that, he didn't make any money at it. Eventually he gave up preaching and became a hermit and a recluse. However, somehow his little maxim about the better mousetrap lived on to become an "oft-quoted" misconception in business literature.

Let's make one thing very clear: If the world is making a beaten path to your door, *your prices are too low.* You want to know how to stave-off the thundering herd? You don't need to call out the National Guard. Just raise your price. Any idiot can cut prices, sell a lot and go broke. Selling occurs when you have the world buying your products and services *even though* your prices are higher than your competitors. It's easy to get people to line-up outside your door when the word on the street is that you are giving your stuff away.

DO YOU REALLY LIKE TO GIVE
YOUR CUSTOMER ANY SERVICE?

Many sales reps (and businesses) really don't like to give their customers any service. In fact, it can probably be argued that *most companies* don't like to give their customers much service. They just figure the only way that you "sell" anything is to be "competitive" -- i.e., have a low price. And they certainly don't seem to accept the idea that service is a responsibility of *all employees* to the customer.

I have a friend who sells carpeting. He, himself, is a very good salesman and manager. A few years ago his company was having trouble with their northwest division. They asked Karl to go out to Seattle and try to shape things up. When he got there, to his amazement, he discovered that this company's customer service telephone number was an *unlisted phone number.*

Now I've been telling that story about the *unlisted customer service telephone number* for several years and you can't really believe the number of, "I've got a better one," stories that I've heard. I think one of the better ones involves an owner of a company who was upset upon discovering that many of his firm's happy customers were using the company's 800 number to call in free to get information about the use and application of his company's products. Feeling that it was a waste of company resources to fund these free telephone calls, this genius-of-selling-skills decided the way to cut down on this "abuse" was to eliminate the 800 number. That, friends, is world-class thinking! However, I should point out that one of the quick-thinkers in the seminar had a suggestion for this guy's boss: Install a 900 phone number, and then the company could actually make money when the customers called in their queries. And, just recently, I had a distributor of chiropractic examination tables tell me that one of his vendors has just taken out his 800 telephone number because, "the only people who ever called us were our customers." So who do you want calling you?

THE SALES REP PERSONIFIES CUSTOMER SERVICE

Many sales reps don't seem to understand the fact that they, in fact, personify customer service. In most business organizations, the only person the customer has ever talked to, perhaps the only person the customer has ever seen, is the sales rep. Whenever anything goes wrong, the only person that the customer can go to is the sales rep. It seems that most companies have all sorts of barricades preventing the customer from talking to anyone other than the sales rep (unless, of course, they have an exceptionally good customer service department).

I have made it my personal avocation to study sales reps that make big dollars. One thing all of them seem to have in common is *they take care of their customers.* They understand that their job as a sales rep is not simply to throw the order in on the desk or into order entry, but to be sure that once the order is entered, that everything occurs as it should. That doesn't mean that they're telling the truck drivers what to do, the warehouse people which orders to pick and ship, the manufacturing people which job to run on which day, or the people in credits and collections and customer service what to do and when. But it does mean that they are watch dogs to ascertain that those things that were *promised* to the customer are actually going to *transpire*: that product is going to be shipped on time, that special information, parts and services are going to be given, that marketing and sales help is going to be provided.

Sales reps who are successful at selling at high prices know that nobody pays big bucks for excuses - nobody! No customer wants to put up with a bunch of lame-brained, half-baked excuses as to why things that were promised did not occur, and they certainly will not tolerate being aggravated and inconvenienced by slip-shod performance upon the part of their vendor. A smart sales rep totally assumes responsibility for bird-dogging, or otherwise pestering those in his/her organization who seem to feel that the customer is a nuisance and that the promises given to the customer really don't have to be fulfilled.

CHAPTER 5

WHY YOU DON'T WANT
TO MESS WITH
PRICE-BUYERS

*"When our vendors were in the
lobby, it looked like they were
waiting for root canal."*
Michael Bozic

Certainly one of the major competitive factors in trying to sell any kind of a product or service has to do with one's success at advertising, promoting and selling the product. And most people will agree that advertising and promoting will help (or hinder) sales of any kind of a product or service. As all the jokes go, 50% of advertising works; the unfortunate thing is that we don't know which 50%.

Presumably advertising and promotion efforts are in the hands of experts in the sales reps' company and those experts know which 50% to use and which 50% not to use -- if that's possible. For purposes of this book, anyway, we shall assume that this is an area over which sales reps have no control. They either benefit from productive promotion or must overcome the unproductive. But I do think I can add something about the selling dimension of this competitive factor and that is this: Sales reps who are most successful DON'T MESS WITH PRICE-BUYERS. That's right -- they know when *not* to sell. There's probably not an experienced sales rep in this country who hasn't had the unhappy experience of taking an order from a customer and, after the fact, wished to hell that he/she had never even met that customer. One of the most difficult things for sales reps to understand is that price-buyers are devoted to the proposition that: "You are not going to make any money on me. Period." So it is incredibly foolhardy for a sales rep to waste time trying to sell to someone with that mindset. The price-buyer is going to squeeze every drop of blood out of the sales rep and the company before they place the order. There's nothing more pathetic than seeing a sales rep trying to nurse an order out of someone who simply has no intention of allowing anyone but himself to "make a buck".

There are fundamentally nine reasons you don't mess with price-buyers. They include:

1. Price–Buyers Take All Your Sales Time.

It is a basic truism that price-buyers take all your sales time. The experienced sales rep should reflect back over the past six months of their selling experience and ask themselves this question: Where have you spent most of your sales time? Inevitably, if you haven't eliminated them, it is with the price-buyer.

Price-buyers have no qualms about wasting your time. Invariably their attitude is, "I've got to get a good deal". They will beat on you and pound on you, ask if you, "can't squeeze a little extra out of here," and, "cut them a deal on this". Then they'll tell you that they need some time to think it over and will ask you perhaps to come back in a couple of weeks, at which time they'll beat on you and pound on you again. A price-buyer has one mentality: We can waste your time or my money. Guess which one they want to waste?

2. They Do All The Complaining.

Price-buyers do all the complaining for two reasons:

a: Complaining builds character in sales reps.

Most price-buyers know that complaining "builds character in sales reps". They've learned long ago from the people who teach negotiation seminars that complaining will almost always get some kind of a price concession or some kind of "special deal" for the buyer. The grounds for this is the logic that most people do not complain unless there is something to complain about. Therefore, most people who hear complaints from their customers figure that they must be really serious or they wouldn't be complaining. Because of this the sales rep is very inclined to say to the boss, "This guy's really unhappy. We better do something about him or we're going to lose this account. Maybe we better cut this guy some kind of a deal to make him happy."

The people who study negotiation skills learn quickly that complaining gets concessions from vendors. Therefore, those who teach negotiation seminars to purchasing agents and buyers teach them to complain. It almost always gets some kind of concession from the selling organization in the form of a discount, rebate, throw-in or some other "extra".

b: They want full measure.

The second reason that many price-buyers do a lot of complaining is that they want full measure. They want "100% satisfaction". But recognize one thing: the customer's notion of "100% satisfaction" will almost always exceed the sales rep's idea of 100% satisfaction. In fact, one might interpret any price-buyer's notion of 100% satisfaction as more like "125% satisfaction".

3. They Forget To Pay You.

One of the interesting things about price-buyers is that once they've told the sales rep that they are "paying good money for this stuff" and "you had better make it right" -- and the sales rep attempts to "make it right" -- then they forget to pay for what they just bought.

It is a provable phenomenon that most price-buyers are slower payers. Anybody to whom money is dear does not settle accounts quickly. Anybody who is willing to beat the daylights out of the sales rep for an extra one quarter of one percent off is more than willing to take that extra discount in the form of the time-value of money by slow pay of their accounts.

One thing that I challenge most people with is this statement: I'll bet I can give you a list of your price-buyers, with 80% accuracy, just by looking at your accounts receivable. Price-buyers are notoriously slow payers and they almost always identify themselves with their payment records.

4. They Tell Your Other Customers How Little They Paid You.

Another one of the problems with price-buyers is that they tell your other customers how little they paid you. Anybody who's proud of their buying skills is sure to brag about what they pay for something. But bragging is an interesting thing. *Bragging does not count unless you are bragging to somebody who appreciates what you are bragging about.*

Consider this scenario: Someone just cut a great deal on a load of sheet rock he bought. Who's he going to brag to about that? His 13-year old son after school? "Sit down, Junior, I'd like to tell you about knocking the soup out of this sales rep on this sheet rock today." The son, of course, will say, "Gee, Pop, that's a terrific story. Tell you what. I'm going to get my buddies in here because they'll want to hear about this, too."

The fact that people brag about what they do is not necessarily bad. But it creates a difficulty for the sales rep who is trying to sell a product at a high price. The reason is that the price-buyer, who cuts a particularly good deal, will run right down the street telling all your other customers how little he/she paid you for something, thereby training your other customers to expect the *same* low price.

In fact, the inevitability that price-buyers will brag about what they've bought and what they paid for something is perhaps the most debilitating thing that a price-buyer can do to their vendor. Not only have they beat up the vendor on price, but they are encouraging other customers to do the same. Therefore, those customers will come at the sales rep with the same kinds of expectations as a price-buyer, thinking that they can get the same terms.

5. *They Drive Off Your Good Customers.*

Price-buyers will often drive off your other good customers. They do this because with all their nagging and complaining and distractions and unwillingness to pay their bill as agreed, etc., they wear down the sales reps to the point that they have little time and energy to give good service to their good customers.

Have you ever had a good day turn sour? Have you ever had a day when you couldn't wait to get home and get your feet up, and you began to realize that it was about 9:15 in the morning that you began to feel that way? Almost always, it is dealing with a price-buyer that makes you feel that way. All they do is tell you about how dumb you are, how stupid you are, how, "they're not going to pay their bill until you do this, that and the other thing," and that, "you've got to make this right," and, "there's a problem with that," and, "you're going to have to fix it before I do anything." Invariably, it is the price-buyer who gets the sales rep psychologically down to the point where they don't feel like dealing with even their good customers.

6. *They're Not Going To Buy From You Again Anyhow.*

Yet another reason that price-buyers cannot be tolerated is because they're not going to buy from you again anyhow. Price-buyers are loyal to only one vendor: the lowest priced. The only way they're going to give you another order is if your price is too low next time and they'll only continue to order from you as long as your prices are too low. They will continue this until such time as your company goes broke, at which time they're going to say, "I knew they were going broke. Their prices were too low. I could have told them that."

It is unfortunately very true that price-buyers have no loyalty to any vendor. You do anything for them, under any conditions, and you can still bet that the minute someone else comes along with a lower price, they're going to jump ship. It is absolutely true that the price-buyer is devoted to the proposition, "You're not going to make any money on me," and appreciates, respects and remembers nothing good that you've ever done for them in the past 4,000 years.

7. *They'll Require You To "Invest Up" To Supply Their Needs – And Then They'll Blackmail You For Yet A Lower Price.*

One of the other things that a price-buyer is apt to do to you is to require you to "invest up" in inventory, land, building, machinery, equipment, trucks, warehouse space, and people to supply their needs. Once they get you fully invested, then they will blackmail you for yet a lower price. They will do that by telling you that they'll have to receive a lower price or otherwise they'll have to "yank all their business" and give it to somebody else. Many larger retailing companies are notorious for having done this over the years. They go to the small manufacturer and give them a big order, watch them increase their inventory, put an addition on their plant, buy new machinery and equipment, hire and train people, and generally "invest up" to supply this big customer's needs. Then, when the big customer has a pretty good idea that the little vendor has need for their volume, they'll blackmail them to receive yet a lower price with the threat of "yanking all of the business" unless some very drastic price concession is made.

Large companies have no particular reason to worry about whether a small vendor fails (other than the short-term inconvenience of changing vendors). They figure there are more fish in the sea and they can always get supplies from someone else. Some of the tragic failures of small businesses have occurred because of the small guy getting suckered in by the big guy and then finding that the big guy simply squeezes out all the blood. It's kind of like the big guy saying, "Which way do you want to die: quick or slow - a bullet between the eyes or a good dose of cancer."

It should be noted that it's not a function of whether or not the customer is a big customer in terms of being a gigantic organization. It's only a question of whether the big customer is big *to the vendor*. If a customer is taking $100,000 in sales, he may not be perceived as a big customer unless the vendor is only doing a million in sales. Then they're taking 10% and that's a lot. My basic precept is this: If you ever have a customer who takes more than 10% of your volume, you are probably vulnerable to this kind of blackmail.

8. They'll Destroy The Credibility of Your Price and Your Product In The Eyes of Your Consumers.

Another major problem of selling to price-buyers at a low price occurs if and when you sell to someone who in turn will resell your product. This is particularly true if you are a manufacturer who sells to a retailer.

If you sell to a retailer who is a price-buyer and they extract a low price from you, you can pretty well bet that they'll turn around and resell your product to the ultimate customer at a low price. Part of the reason for this is that they feel that all customers buy on price largely because they, themselves, buy on price. And they know if they can get you to cut them a low price deal, then they can turn around and resell at a low price deal and presumably still maintain their margins.

The problem with them reselling your product at a low price is that they destroy the credibility of your product and the price of your product in the eyes of your consumer. The retailer who buys at a low price and then resells at a low price is in essence telling the ultimate consumer (the public) that this product is not

46

worth the big price that others are paying for it. After all, if it was worth much, it would cost more. Any number of the "discounters" and "clubs" and "wholesale outlets" and other nationally known discount retail operations have completely destroyed manufacturers of products by doing this. The technical term for this is known as *whoring up the market.*

9. *They will steal any ideas, designs, drawings, information, and knowledge they can get their hands on.*

Price-buyers often have little or no scruples when it comes to stealing anything they can get their hands (or brains) on. They will ask you to "show them you can do it" or "prove you have the talent" or "give us your ideas and then we'll think about it." And when they say "give", they mean *GIVE.*

You are foolish to fall for these ideas about developing a relationship with a customer by proving yourself unless they are willing to pay for your ideas. That is why we have patent and copyright laws. See pp. 162 - 164 for the two ways you protect yourself from this theft. And never forget this admonition -- if your ideas are worth anything, they must be paid for.

DELIVERY - THE ULTIMATE IN COMPETITIVE ADVANTAGE

The other thing that you can compete on is called delivery, which is the ability to put the product in the customer's hot little hand, when and where he needs it. Delivery is handily the one thing you *must* be competitive on if you want to sell at a higher price than your competitor. In many industries, a company's ability to deliver (or their inability to deliver) may make or break them.

Have you ever wondered why your customer goes to all the trouble to explain to you that they can go down the street and get the same thing at a lower price? If they can really get it cheaper down the street, why don't they go down the street and get it? Why do they waste all that time telling you, "I can get it cheaper down the street." The reason is two-fold. One is because they *can't* -- and they are lying about the price or your competitor's ability to deliver the product on time and/or it really isn't the same stuff. What they are really saying is: I want *that guy's* price -- but I want *your* ability to deliver, *your* investment in inventory, *your* way of doing business, *your* service, *your* quality, *your* people, *your* investment in machinery and equipment. The second is because they can get it, *but they don't want to, better not*, or *can't* because "they" (your competitor) won't sell it to them. Let's analyze this.

When a customer tells you they can "get the same stuff down the street, for less money," you always want to ask yourself this question: Why are they talking to me? If they can get *the same stuff* down the street, *right now*, for less money, why are they talking to me?

REASONS CUSTOMERS DON'T GET IT
DOWN THE STREET FOR A CHEAPER PRICE:

REASON #1. They Can't Get It
- A. They are lying about the price.
- B. The same stuff isn't available now.
- C. It isn't the same stuff.

REASON #2. They Can *But*
- A. They don't want to get it there.
- B. They better not get it there.
- C. For some reason, they can't (even though it is available) because your competitor won't sell it to them.

THEY CAN'T GET IT

• THEY LIE ABOUT THE PRICE

I hope this observation doesn't burst too many readers' balloons, but customers do lie, especially when it is to their advantage. One lie that many customers tell is about the price. They simply state that the other guy's price is lower when it is not. Also, they sometimes "stretch the truth". They claim that the other guy's price is lower because of "other things" that the other guy will do -- i.e., your

48

competitor will pay the freight or give better terms, etc. Or they will do the reverse -- insist that the other guy's price ($98) is lower than your price ($100) when they know that the *real* price is not lower. For example, let's say your price is $100, but you pay the freight, give credit for 30 days, and will ship to all four of your customer's job sites at no extra charge. Furthermore, you will sell in less than case lots. Your competitor, whose price is $98, is cheaper -- says your customer -- totally overlooking the fact that your competitor's $98 price is COD, and that furthermore your competitor will not sell in less than case lots, will pay no freight and will do no shipping to job sites. So whose price is really cheaper?

Another form of lying that your customer will do is to actually counterfeit or forge your competitor's quotations, thereby "substantiating" your competitor's lower prices. Today's high-tech copy machines make this form of fraud child's play. I talked to a purchasing agent in California several years ago who bragged to me about not only how simple such fraud was to do, but how effectively it worked.

• THE SAME STUFF ISN'T AVAILABLE AT THIS TIME

Marvin Schutt, the late executive director of the National Sporting Goods Association, used to tell the following story to make this point. Seems that this guy comes into a sporting goods store and wants to buy a can of tennis balls. "How much are your tennis balls?" he says.

The merchant says, "They're $3.50 a can."

The customer says, "$3.50! Why I can get the exact same can of tennis balls down the street at your competitors for a buck and a half."

"Well, I'm sorry sir, I can't let you have it at that price," says the merchant. "I guess you'll have to go down there and get them."

"Well, I would, but I can't," replies the customer.

"Why can't you?" asks the merchant.

"Well, he's out of tennis balls right now," says the customer.

49

"Oh, well, you come back when I'm out. Mine are only a buck a can when I'm out. I'll give you a helluva deal when I'm out," retorted the merchant.

Many salespeople really don't appreciate how important delivery is. They do not seem to understand that, usually, when a customer is saying that they can get it cheaper, what they're trying to do is to get *your* quality, service and delivery *at the other guy's price.* Because if they can really get a better deal, they would be down there *getting it* and wouldn't be wasting their time trying to con you into cutting your price.

You can't find a retail sales clerk with any experience who hasn't seen the above scenario played out. You learn quickly, if you are a good judge of actions instead of words, that if the customer could really get a better deal (quality, service and on-time delivery) that the customer would be down the street buying it, and not be wasting time telling the sales rep how much better a deal they "can" get at the competitors.

- IT ISN'T THE SAME STUFF

Yet another lie that your customer will tell you about being able to get the same stuff down the street for less money is that it simply is not the same stuff. It is easy to say that "the same stuff" is the same stuff even though the quantity, size, quality, color, weight, performance characteristics, volume, shape, taste, feel, smell, range, power, texture, etc., etc., etc. isn't even close. It is the sales rep's job to know (or verify) what the competition is offering and not fall for such lies as these.

THEY CAN GET IT, BUT...

The second reason your customer will spend a lot of time telling you he can get the same stuff down the street, cheaper, is that he can *BUT.* But what?

- HE DOESN'T WANT TO

It is easy to say, "I can get the same stuff down the street for less money," especially when you can. But, often, what the customer knows is that, although he can get the identically *same stuff* for less money *right now* he doesn't really

50

want to. Why not? Because you (and/or your company) are better and easier to do business with; you are more reliable and easier to work with; you have better service, better hours, better trained people; you have quicker order turnaround time, give a better warranty or guarantee, honor your commitments, have more compatible systems of accounting, invoicing, record keeping, etc., etc., etc. In short, many customers will tell you, truthfully, that they can get it cheaper -- but they really know that you and your company offer the best buy. They just want you to cut your own price -- even though they are going to buy from you anyway.

•   HE BETTER NOT BUY IT THERE

What do you mean he better not buy it there? He better not -- because the boss said so. Many a customer can tell you, truthfully, that he can get the same stuff from your competitor for less money. The part he won't tell you, of course, is that he better not buy it there because someone very powerful in the company suggested to him that he better not get it there, for whatever good reason. And usually the people who flex that kind of muscle (A) have good reason for doing so, (B) accept no other sources and (C) know that savings of a few dollars "over there" is just plain stupid.

•   THEY CAN'T GET IT THERE, EVEN THOUGH IT'S AVAILABLE

The third reason that a customer will tell you that he can get it down the street cheaper is that they can't, even though they can. This is not double talk. Truth is, even when it is a widely known fact that your competitor is offering the same stuff at less money and can deliver it, your customer can't buy it from your competitor *because your competitor won't sell it to him.* Why won't your competitor sell it to him? Lots of reasons:

A)   Your prospective customer is a jerk -- lies, steals, takes advantage, difficult person to deal with, sets up too many obstacles for ease of doing business, etc.

B)   Your prospective customer hasn't paid for the last stuff he bought -- a point which will only surprise the most naive reader.   And let me give a little philosophical thought here -- if you aren't going to be paid for it, either, you ought to charge more for it.

C)   Your competitor won't sell it to your prospective customer as a matter of policy. Many buyers for governmental agencies face this problem -- potential vendors won't even give them a quote, let alone write up the order for them.

Your customer certainly will try to get you to cut your price, and will tell you they can get the same stuff, down the street, for less money. But if that were true, why would they spend any real time telling you about this better deal? The point is, you should always learn to waste this customer's time (professionally, of course) and see how hard he works at telling you he can get the same stuff, cheaper. If he can -- you are history. The reason he'll spend time telling you he can, but doesn't run you off, is because he can't or, if he can, he doesn't want to or better not.

As we said above, delivery is the trigger event that will cause loss of sales in 70% of the situations when you lose a sale to an existing customer. Conversely, ability to deliver the right stuff at the right place at the right time with good service will get you sales. Frankly, of all the things that a company can compete on, the singularly most significant, most important, is delivery. If your company has a delivery problem, it will have difficulty in selling *at any price*, let alone a *high* price. If your company has a bad track record on delivery (or quality or service) your company will start losing sales. Anybody can cut price, get an increase in sales volume, foul-up delivery, have quality problems develop, find their service going to Hades, and go broke. Product is sold -- and prices stick -- because a business gives its customers quality, service, and on-time delivery. And those companies know how to advertise, promote and sell those points about doing business with them. But all those things cost money. If you are going to give your customer what they *need* and *want*, you've got to charge a high price. The good news is you can succeed in doing that. That is why those companies who have historically charged higher prices have (A) survived the longest, (B) made the most money and (C) have been able to pay the highest wages, salaries and commissions to the people who work for them.

CHAPTER 6

WHAT BUYERS AND CUSTOMERS *REALLY NEED.* HINT -- IT ISN'T LOW PRICE

"If your customer truly needs a low price, you can't afford to sell to him."
Cletus Peichl

Most companies go broke because they believe they can sell low and make it up in volume. In this book we have shown that those companies that seem to be successful are companies that charge high prices, but know how to *sell* their product. However, the ability to sell isn't just a function of salesmanship -- and it really isn't a function of highest quality (although, admittedly, it is very difficult to peddle genuine junk for very long and survive). What does a customer really need? What do they really buy? Someone who is really a buyer, or functioning in that capacity, must have some things. What are they?

Many sales reps succumb to buyer pressures to get them to cut their prices because they have never analyzed what the customer *needs* versus what he says he needs [wants]. Buyers do not need a low price. They will tell you they do, they may even think they do, and they certainly have a lot of pressure to try to get a low price. But they don't *need* a low price. In fact, if they truly *need* a low price, you better not take their order -- they may not be able (or willing) to pay you. Let's examine some of the things that buyers really need:

1. They Need Two Or More Vendors.

Sole-sourcing is very perilous. Even if there are thousands of vendors, sole-sourcing is dumb. This is because any business can have a fire, flood, tornado, hurricane, earthquake, volcanic eruption, labor strike, failure of their vendors to ship to them on time or, as happened to a business in Denver not so long ago, the Immigration and Naturalization Service came in and took all of its employees. They took every production employee it had, and guess who its major customer was? The U.S. Government. Well, that caused the business to miss delivery. And the government, of course, penalized the business for late delivery. But they took all of its employees. Of course, the government's attitude was that the business shouldn't have had those employees to begin with. And the business owner's reponse was; "I had those employees because you wanted a low price."

Sole-sourcing is stupid and most buyers can't afford it. For example, many people argue that the Federal government is a real price-buyer, but even they have rules and regulations against sole-sourcing. Even if there are many, many vendors, sole-sourcing is dangerous because if one sole-sources and something happens to that source, one must quickly -- and I mean overnight -- come up with another source. This is not always so easy to do, especially if you're dealing with large volumes. If you don't have a track record, if you don't have a history of good payment, if you don't have an on-going relationship, those other vendors may not sell to you. They don't know you, don't need you, they have managed to get along without you as a customer up to now, so why should they help you? And if they've ever tried to deal with you in the past, they may not trust you.

Buyers learn fairly early in the game that sole-sourcing is very dangerous. So most won't do it. That means, by definition, that one vendor can charge a higher price than the lowest price bidder. Also, virtually all customers who buy in bid situations reserve the right to reject any and all bids. This is because they know that if they accept the lowest bid they are vulnerable to any idiot who writes down a very small number on a piece of paper, gets the bid, and then fails to perform.

2. They Need On-Time Delivery.

More than anything else, buyers need on-time delivery. If you can deliver on time, you don't have to sell at the lowest price. If you can't deliver on time, forget about commanding a higher price -- and with the possible exception of short term, forget about selling at any price. (More to come on this later in Chapter 8 , but keep this in mind: many businesses have delivery problems because they have gotten too much business because their prices are too low.)

3. They Like Reinforcement Of The Idea That They're Doing Something -- That They're Cutting A Deal.

For any readers who are in a negotiated bid situation (versus sealed bids), a couple of points you must remember is that many buyers think they must "cut a deal". In other words, they don't want to just be "order placers". In these situations, false pricing is the only solution. This generally works because of the way purchasing people are paid: i.e. virtually none are paid (or rewarded) on how little they *spend*, but on how much they *save*. Thus, if you ask a significantly higher price than your competition, but tell your customer you can "knock more off" than your competition, you still have a higher selling price, but one that shows the customer having bigger "savings" by buying from you than by buying from your competitor. The following illustrates how this can work:

Let's say you're selling Fords and your competitor is selling Chevys; you're asking $10,000 for your car and your competitor is asking $9200. But let's say you're willing to take (in a negotiated bid) $9000 for your Ford -- and your competitor is willing to take $8800. You have an excellent shot at getting the sale at the $9000 price, over your competitor's $8800. Why? Because if you're selling your Ford, asking $10,000, but willing to take $9000, you can give your customer a $1000 saving. If your competitor is asking $9200, but will go to $8800, he can only give his customer a $400 saving.

Now some of you probably feel that I don't understand: the real "savings" is $200; between the $9000 and $8800. Yes, but you can't prove that saving to your boss if you are a buyer. After all, a Ford isn't a Chevy. You can't say I saved $200 because I bought a Chevy -- *because you can't prove that.* While a Ford may be very similar to a Chevy, it isn't a Chevy. Even if they have all of the same features and options, the cars aren't identical. *You can prove* you saved $1000 by buying the Ford, but you only saved $400 if you bought the Chevy.

Whenever you have a negotiated bid situation where you have a differentiable item, false pricing works. I personally don't like to do it, but it does work. If you ask a falsely high price, or at least a higher price than your competitors, and are willing to negotiate a wider spread, the purchasing agent is hard put to refuse it because by buying from you he can report to the boss, "Hey, when I bought those four new Fords I saved $4000. Had I bought those four new Chevys, I would only have saved $1600."

Incidentally, the reciprocal of the above (that you might successfully use false pricing because of how purchasing agents and buyers are paid) is the fact that you should never, as a sales rep, tell a purchasing agent, customer or buyer how you are paid; this is particularly relevant if you're paid by commission. The reason for this is because if they know you're paid a commission, they know you are motivated to sell at a low price. Why? Because something beats nothing all to hell. Let's say you are paid a 7% commission rate. If you sell $100 worth of product, your commission is $7. If you sell it at only $90, your commission is only $6.30. Granted, you're going to make more money if you sell at $100 but you may not get the sale at $100 and 7% of nothing is nothing. Most anybody would rather get $6.30 in commission than get nothing. And that is why, if you are paid a commission on your sales dollars, you are motivated to sell at a low price.

Purchasing agents know how the foregoing works. If you tell them you're paid commission, they figure that you're more desperate to sell at any price, under the theory that something beats nothing all to hell. So never tell them you're paid commission. If they ask you how you're paid, or try to wheedle it out of you, do the right thing: lie. Tell them you're paid salary and you've got a 50-year contract that's non-cancellable. It's none of their business how you're paid, anyhow. Another thing you should never tell a customer is that you've got a contest going (and that you and your spouse are going to get a free trip to Hawaii if you sell another $40,000 worth this month). Once a customer knows you *really* want (need) a sale, they'll know you are willing to give away the store at any price, just to run up your sales volume and qualify for that free trip.

4. They Need Respect.

Sure, we all need respect. Give them a little, and they might think about buying from you.

5. They Need Help And Guidance On Complex Purchases.

Here is your real chance to sell. People who do buying often are not knowledgeable about what they are buying. If you, as a sales rep, see your role as an educator and teacher to a harried purchasing agent, you can get a leg up on your competition. A lot of sales reps seem to think that selling is just telling jokes, being friendly and finding out the other guy's price so they can slide in under it. They don't work at educating their customers and don't give that dimension of sales service that gets the respect and loyalty of the customer. Don't ever expect a customer to buy from loyalty. But recognize that if you are a knowledgeable, helpful representative of your company's products, you will always have access to the ears of your customers. This gives you the opportunity to present the reasons that they should pay you a premium price, which is that you not only have helped educate them about what to buy, but have been able to explain about your ability to deliver the kind of quality product they need, on time, and can back up your order with impeccable service.

6. They Need To Buy What They Are Told To Buy.

Buyers and purchasing agents need to buy what they are *told* to buy. People in buying and purchasing agent jobs don't very often decide what to buy -- no matter what they tell you. Studies show that 85% of the time the person doing the buying job in a business has little or no say in what they buy; in fact, in 32% of the cases, they have *no* say in the purchase decision. Don't ever forget this because that fact substantiates the need to do back-door selling. Purchasing agents, of course, hate back-door selling because it works. Now some of you will react negatively to this suggestion. You'll think: "Hey, man, don't talk to me about back-door selling -- you try that and you'll get thrown out in the snow." In fact, the January 1987 *Small Business Report*[12], states that:

> "Purchasing managers indicated they do not like a sales person who practices back-door selling; that is, by-passes the purchasing manager to talk directly with the end user of the product. Thirty-

---

[12]   *Small Business Report*, January, 1987.

six percent of them complained about that."

That's why you want to do it!! It works!!

It's like playing any sport or activity where there is any adversarial game or challenge. If they don't want you to go there, that's where you want to go! If they don't care whether you go there, there's no point in going. The trick to this approach is that you've got to learn how to tactfully and diplomatically do back-door selling. Purchasing agents and buyers will definitely resent it. They resent it because it is so incredibly successful. And, remember, if you don't do it, your competition probably is!

Later in this book we're going to talk about purchasing agent tricks, one of which is that they try to stiff-arm the sales rep -- i.e., they say, "We can't pay any more than $18." This is your open invitation to do back-door selling. Just ask "Why?" They'll inevitably say, "Because my boss (or whoever) said so." When they tell you because "so and so" said so, they are pointing out the individual to whom you should go to sell; they are fingering the individual who is the decision maker. Learn to use that knowledge . This is when you say, "Gee, I can't believe they said that." Or, "I'm sure they want to get the right stuff. Maybe I should talk to them?"

Back-door selling is incredibly persuasive, but if you do it poorly, you are going to get thrown out in the snow. So you have to learn how to do it diplomatically. Not just because in 32% of the situations a purchasing agent has no say in what they buy and you must sell to decision makers, but because, while it's in only 32% of the situations in which they have no say, those situations *cover 68% of the dollars spent*. In other words, the bigger the ticket, the higher the probability that the purchasing agent has no say in what they buy, so you must get to the decision maker for bigger ticket sales. Also remember that big tickets come in two ways: (A) it is a very expensive item, or (B) it is a cheap item, but they must buy lots of them.

Back-door selling works because people other than purchasing agents or buyers have sway, or some say, in what is bought. The guys in engineering, the plant manager, the people who are going to use the product in application -- all have a lot to do with the purchase decision, maybe everything. You've got to learn where that power play is. A good example of this (where it is virtually an art form) is the way commercials for the Saturday morning kiddie shows are used. Why do you think they advertise cereal on those shows? It's not because little kids have a concern about the nutritional value of what they're eating. No. It's because the advertisers are trying to persuade the *decision maker* (the kid) to tell the *purchasing agent* (the parent) to go out and get the right cereal. That's all there is to it.

Many sales reps forget this Iron Law of back-door selling: forgiveness is far easier to get than is permission. Don't ask for permission to do back-door selling, just do it. You can seldom get permission, but almost always, you can get forgiveness.

7. They Need To Get What They Buy - Quantity, Quality, Timeliness.

They need to get what they've ordered. They need to have it on hand, in place, so that they don't have to shut the place down. This is just another paragraph on the critical importance of your ability to deliver product to your customer, on time, in top condition.

8. They Need To Minimize Inventory Carrying Costs Without Jeopardizing The Company's Needs.

Your customer (or purchasing agent or buyer) needs "just-in-time inventory" -- nothing late, not too much on hand. This is a tough requirement, and if they can be assured that you can deliver on time you have a strong selling advantage. Any astute business needs to try to minimize inventory carrying costs. But understand one thing: all this business about statistical quality control, this high pressure to have "just-in-time" delivery, emphasizes the importance of one thing: *DELIVERY*, not price. They'll tell you they want low price, but they'll *cut you off* as a vendor if you screw-up delivery.

9. They Need To Buy From A Technically Current And Financially Sound Vendor.

Any of you want to buy a ticket on People Express Airlines today? They sure were cheap. Yeah, but they're OOB (Out-Of-Business). Ever try to buy from any company that went out-of-business? It's very hard to do; but the price is (was) right, isn't (wasn't) it? Most low price competitors go broke quick. People Express Airlines, for example, went from nothing in sales to more than $1,000,000 000 in sales and back to nothing in only five years time. One day they may be out there selling and the next day the doors are locked, the phones shut off, etc. Most purchasing agents learn early in the game that you've got to buy from whoever is going to deliver quality product, on time. If they don't they're going to be in a job-threatening situation when the company doesn't have the needed materials. Any smart purchasing agent or buyer is far more concerned over the probability of you being able to deliver on time, than they are about your low price.

10. *They Need More Certainty On A Items (compared to B or C items).*

A items, of course, are items a company must *never* be without. B items are important and there should never be any problem on availability. C items are so ubiquitous that we don't need to worry about them. Customers need A items; items that are really critical to their business. For example, an airline needs fuel (A item) more than they need ice (B item). Now, some of the drinkers might not agree with that, but most drinkers will agree that they would rather run out of ice than out of fuel, particularly at 30,000 feet. However, if they run out of cocktail stirers (C item) probably no one will get too upset. Thus, lack of B and C items will not put the airline out-of-business, but lack of item A spells major disaster for the company.

11. *They Need Production/Performance Capable Vendors.*

Here again, is the old, delivery factor. If you simply do not have the capability (capacity, know-how, experience) to get the product to your customer, on time, in good shape, you aren't going to get the order no matter how good your price. One can see this clearly in bid situations when the low bidder doesn't get the job because the people letting the bid are afraid that bidder can't perform to specifications.

12. *They Need Courtesy, Speed And Timely Action Upon The Part Of The Sales Reps In Accepting Orders, Answering Questions, Responding To Order Problems Or Delays.*

It's amazing the number of sales people that don't want to talk to their customers. It is not unusual to hear sales reps call in for messages and, when told they have none, they say "Great!" If they do have some, they may say, "Well, did he want me to call today?" or, "Do you think it was important?" or, "Tell him you weren't able to reach me, but you'll make sure that I'll call him later."

13. They Need Speed And Accuracy In Invoicing And Help On Cost Information.

I have a friend in the public seminar business who gave me an example of how important such minor things as fast and accurate invoicing can be. He said, "I cut-off one of my vendors, a printer. You want to know why? Because he wouldn't itemize what various cuts and folds were costing and I could not make a decision as to whether or not I wanted to continue with a certain brochure and the other things that I was doing. I think this guy thought I was trying to figure out where he was getting ahead of me on price, but that wasn't my motive. My problem was, I wanted to know if this special fold I was using was worth doing. He wasn't trying to beat me on the price, I don't think, although it was a negotiated bid. But he couldn't (or wouldn't) tell me the break-out on the cost so that I could make an intelligent business decision. I just decided I couldn't afford to do business with him. And then this printer called me up and wanted to know if his price was too high? I said, "No, your service is no good. And I don't want to do business with you!"

14. They Need Vendor Order And Sales Service Department Help.

I talked to a contractor who developed shopping centers and he told me that one of his biggest problems was getting sales service and information from sales reps, especially when he was getting into something in which he had little knowledge or experience. The example he used was in trying to get information on automatic doors (at entry ways for supermarkets -- or motels/hotels or airports) that he needed to install. The concern was over safety, product liability and the maintenance of such doors. Apparently the sales service people he talked to didn't think that those questions were important; that the fact that they could offer him the lowest prices was what he needed to know or, at least, so they thought. He said he didn't buy from the lower price guys, but rather bought from the one company that gave him the answers (and assurances) about his concerns.

15. They Need Quality Transportation Carriers Used By Vendors.

If you ship good product, but it shows up broken or unuseable, you either have a transportation carrier problem or a packaging problem. If it leaves your place in good shape, but it gets torn up in transit, it's because whoever is shipping it tore it up or (and this is most commonly the case), you didn't package it right for the type of transportation carrier you used. In either event, you still have a delivery or a quality problem. Understand that failure to get a quality product in the hands of your customer on time is almost a sure-fire way to lose a customer -- not because of your price, but because the product can't be used when it gets there (or it is too much trouble to use) and your customer will start looking for another vendor.

DELIVERY - YOU CAN'T SELL AT A HIGH PRICE WITHOUT IT

Delivery is incredibly significant in your ability to sell at a high price. The good news is, *if you raise your price*, you probably can eliminate your delivery problems, improve your gross margin, profitability and earn bigger commissions and bonuses -- even though your competitors have a lower price than you do. The reason low price vendors have delivery problems is that in order to sell at a low price, they have to cut back on everything. The volume which may be created by the low price usually results in an inability to produce enough product on time. The first thing that happens is they get late on shipments. Then, of course, because of "hurry up", quality gets bad. With poor quality, customer complaints start rolling in, and then service goes to hell. Planned sales volume of quality goods, with on-time delivery, means that you can sell at a higher price than your competitors.

CHAPTER 7

THINGS BUYERS WOULD LIKE
BESIDES A LOW PRICE

*"The bitterness of poor quality
remains long after the sweetness
of low price is forgotten."*
Anonymous

We have already established that the customer will tell you he needs a lower price, but that isn't true. What he needs are the things we outlined in the foregoing chapter. If he truly needs a low price, you can't afford to sell to that customer.

Of course, your customer would like a low price. But he's probably realistic enough to understand that he's going to get what he pays for and, if he buys from the low price competitor, he will probably let himself in for a great many problems -- some of which will be ultimately intolerable. So don't ever try to compete on low price; rather concentrate your efforts on providing the customer with what he needs and, of course, charge an appropriate (high) price for that performance on your part.

Customers like a lot of other things besides low price, and some of these other things can be just as persuasive as low price in getting your customer to buy.

Let's take a look at some of the things that you can provide to customers to get them to buy from you at a price higher than your competitors.

BUYERS' LIKES

Buyers like a lot of things. Some of those things include the following:

• AN EASY "NO BRAINER" RELATIONSHIP.

People are people. When it's easy to do business with someone, it makes the other person's life better. If you can provide your customers with an easy relationship in which they get what they want, when they need it, on time and in good shape, you'll probably find it easier to make that sale at a higher price .

• RELIABILITY AND DEPENDABILITY.

People like to know that they can rely on you. This almost always comes from the history of the relationship. It is a foolish (and rare) customer who will drop a known vendor to save a few pennies to buy from an unknown vendor. When customers tell you they can get it cheaper down the street, you might remind them that they know they can rely upon you and that there may be a serious question mark down the street.

• PREDICTABILITY.

Customers not only like reliability, they like predictability. Your predictability is based upon your past relationship. Most people who study behavior of any sort know one thing -- what someone has done in the past pretty well indicates what they'll do in the future. Again, if you've got good marks in your past relationship, you've probably got an edge over your competition on future relationships.

• REACTION TO THEIR NEEDS.

Most people like to think of themselves as being a little bit "different". "You don't understand, our business is different from those other guys," is a very common refrain of many buyers. And, to some degree, they are virtually always right. Therefore, a way to ingratiate yourself in the eyes of your prospective customer is to be very flexible and responsive to their specialized needs. Such flexibility virtually always warrants a purchase order, even at a higher price.

64

- SHORT DELIVERY TIMES.

Even those customers who do not aggressively pursue the concept of "just-in-time" delivery, still like short delivery times. Everybody wants it yesterday. Companies who sell at premium prices certainly will cater to these likes of the customers and try to provide quick turn-around times between the placing of the order and the delivery of the product.

- HELP AT REDUCING COSTS BY REALIZING SAVINGS.

The customer would like you to help them in accomplishing their goal of minimizing their costs and realizing economies in their operations to enhance their company's bottom line. Anything you can do to help them realize genuine savings will be appreciated. But I don't think that by cutting your price you're going to help them realize a genuine saving -- particularly if your company goes broke and fails to deliver as promised and creates all kinds of havoc for them. Recognize that genuine help has to do with advice and assistance relative to uses and applications of your products and services in the hands of your customer, not just giving a low price.

- BREADTH AND DEPTH IN QUALITY.

Customers like to know that historically the vendor has had breadth and depth in their quality programs. Your customer wants you to react to their needs. That means that they want you to not only have breadth, but also depth in your ability to react to the things they're trying to accomplish by buying your product or service. That especially has to do with seeing to it that they are getting the right quality and maximum utilization of the products and services they're buying from you.

- TOTAL PRODUCT OFFERINGS.

It is very inconvenient to have to use six or eight vendors for different products when one or two will do. A complete line or a full offering simply makes it easier for the buyer to accomplish this goal -- getting the right stuff in the organization at the right place at the right time. A full product line often gets orders simply because of the ease and convenience associated with buying from one company rather than a variety of sources.

- KNOWLEDGE, COMPETENCE AND FOLLOW-UP ON THE SALES REP'S PART.

We all like to know that "we're in good hands". Sales reps who are serious about following up on orders, making sure that everything's right and, in general, are quite thorough in processing things after the order is received, find that this activity gives them an opportunity to sell at a preferential price.

- WILLINGNESS OF THE SALES REP TO "GO TO BAT" FOR THE BUYER WHEN PROBLEMS ARISE.

Your customers would like to have somebody in their corner, on their side. Your customers will appreciate -- and likely pay a premium price for -- genuine help if and when any kind of problem arises. Certainly your customers expect you to work for them -- even though your employer is the one who pays your commission or salary. You can win customers for life when you are willing to help them in those crisis situations.

- SALES REPS THAT KNOW THEIR PRODUCT LINE.

Your customers expect you to know what you're selling. That means that you can assist them in making the best choice in buying what it is that they want or expect to buy from you. If you don't know your own product line, you're not going to be very convincing to a customer as to why he/she should buy from you -- particularly at a premium price.

- SALES REPS THAT KNOW THE BUYER'S PRODUCT LINE.

Not only do your customers expect you to know your own line, they expect you to know their (the buyer's) product line or business. How can you help them if you don't know what it is they're trying to do? How can you expect to convince them to buy your products or services from you when you don't know what uses and applications they will be making with that product if they do buy it from you?

- SALES REPS WHO ARE PREPARED FOR THEIR SALES CALLS.

There are an awful lot of sales reps who simply "wing it", and if you're a real talker, a genuine word merchant, you may have a problem as a sales rep because you figure you can always "fake it". If you don't prepare for your sales call (i.e., understand your customer's products and services, and how they expect to use your product or service) you've got big problems if you expect someone to pay you a premium price.

- SALES REPS WHO MAKE REGULAR, PREDICTABLE SALES CALLS.

People like predictability. People who do buying like to know that the sales rep will come around on a regular, predictable basis. The sales rep who shows up on a hit or miss basis is not perceived as being reliable and is thus viewed as a questionable source of supply. Nobody pays a premium price to a questionable vendor.

THE LOWEST BIDDER

"It's unwise to pay too much, but it is worse to pay too little. When you pay too much, you lose a little money -- that's all. When you pay too little, you sometimes lose everything, because the thing you bought was incapable of doing the thing it was bought to do. The common law of business balance prohibits paying a little and getting a lot -- it can't be done. If you deal with the lowest bidder, it is well to add something for the risk you run. And if you do that, you will have enough to pay for something better."
John Ruskin (1819 - 1900)

- TECHNICAL EDUCATION ABOUT WHAT THEY ARE BUYING, IF RELEVANT.

Not all products that are bought by buyers or purchasing agents are technical. But many buyers have to buy things that are technical. The sales rep who will provide that purchasing agent or buyer with a little technical education may very well get that preferential nod when it comes to getting the order at a premium over the competitor's prices.

- INFREQUENT SHORT SHIPMENTS.

Most people who buy things are realists. Sometimes, problems come up. Nobody likes non-delivery, but probably very few people expect 100% delivery 100% of the time for eternity. Normally when a business can't ship a complete quantity, they will engage in short shipments. This is probably acceptable to most customers, assuming that the short shipment is enough to allow them to get

67

through until the full order is received. But nobody likes to be on pins and needles worrying about whether or not the rest of the shipment is going to get there on time. And nobody likes to put up with frequent short shipments, even though ultimately everything has worked out in the past. There is still the worry factor and nobody pays big bucks to have to worry about a vendor delivering on time.

• EASE OF INTERPRETATION OF VENDOR PRICE-LISTS AND QUOTES.

Another thing that buyers like is ease of interpreting the price that the sales rep is charging. If you, as a sales rep, can clearly point out to the customer exactly what the price is in simple, understandable terms, you're more apt to get the order. If customers have to figure out 87 different things to ascertain the real price, their apt to give their business to the sales rep who makes it a simple, quick, clean and honest quotation. Confusion is not trusted, and people and companies who are not trusted aren't paid premium prices.

• EARLY NOTICE OF SHIPMENT PROBLEMS.

If you ever have a shipping problem, let your customer know it well before hand. That, at least, will give them the opportunity to cover themselves with some other source of the product or materials. Of course, it's hard to maintain customers when you force them to look for other sources, but it's probably impossible to retain them when you screw them up royally and give them a nasty surprise. If you want to retain a customer, and you're going to have a shipment problem, let them know up front how you are going to help them get through the difficulty.

• ADVANCE WARNING OF DISCONTINUANCE OF ITEMS.

Again, people don't like surprises. If your company is going to discontinue a product or service that your customer has been using, they'd like to know in ample time to cover their own self-interests relative to the pending unavailability of that product or service. Can they phase out their inventory? Can they avoid building an advertising campaign around your product that isn't going to be available for them to resell? Can they avoid the expense of designing your product into their equipment and then discovering that it's no longer available for them to use in building their equipment? When your customer knows that you'll be on top of things and keep them alert, you'll find that getting that special order at a premium price is a lot easier.

• UNDERSTANDABLE, AND LEGIBLE, SHIPPING DOCUMENTS. Not only do people like to get clear quotes and easy-to-understand invoices, they also like to have understandable and legible shipping documents. Most people who buy things have to receive those things. Experience tells them (because of the unreliability of many sellers) that they had better compare what they received with what they were supposed to receive and what they are going to be billed for. The more your organization can do to keep that dimension of purchasing a simpler matter will again enhance the probability that you will get preferential treatment when it comes to selling your product.

CHAPTER 8

YOUR COMPETITORS' DELIVERY PROBLEMS WILL GET YOU PROFITABLE SALES

"Without a guarantee, customers won't complain – or come back."
Christopher W. L. Hart

When your competitors get delivery, quality or service problems, their customers start looking for other vendors. And when a customer cuts off one vendor because of delivery, quality and/or service and replaces that vendor with a new vendor, how do they pick the new vendor? On the basis of price? Of course, not. When they are qualifying a new source, what is going to be the single, most important question they will ask? Am I going to get what I need when I want it? When those purchasing agents, buyers and customers start asking you questions about your ability to deliver quality product, on time, and back it up with great service, you need to be able to *prove* to your customer that you can perform. You need to assure them that you can get what they need, where they want it, when they need it, without any excuses.

THE ECONOMICS OF PRICING

Let's have a quick lesson in the economics of pricing. Most business people (let alone most sales people) don't seem to understand how selling at a high price ties in with a customer's decision to buy at a higher price.   That is because sales types (and other business executives) often have no idea how much volume of product sales is required to make up for a price cut, or how much loss of product sales can be tolerated in the event of a price increase.

In Econ 101, or some such theoretical course, they told you that you, "could cut price and make it up in volume." I even had one instructor tell me that I could cut my price 10% and would only need to increase my sales volume by 10% to make up for the price cut. Well, that might be true if I had a 92% gross margin. But you want to know something -- I haven't found many businesses yet that have a 92% gross margin.

In the real world, if you cut your price 10%, your company will probably have to at least *double* what it's currently selling, and might even have to triple it or more. Let me prove this to you. First, pick a product that you sell.   Now ask yourself this: If I cut my price 10%, how much more volume do I have to sell of that product to make up for the 10% price cut?

If you don't have an answer for that question, then you have no business negotiating prices with your customer, or even commenting on the appropriateness of your product's price, *because you don't know what you're doing!* I want to show you how to answer that question for yourself. You've got to understand what happens in your business if you start fooling around cutting price rather than learning to sell on some basis besides low price.

THE VOLUME SWINGS ASSOCIATED WITH PRICE CUTTING: HOW TO DETERMINE HOW MUCH MORE YOU MUST SELL TO MAKE UP FOR A PRICE CUT -- AND HOW MUCH LESS YOU NEED TO SELL IF YOU RAISE PRICES

Many sales people have no idea how to figure out what happens to the amount of volume of a product a company must sell if it cuts price. They just seem to think that, somehow, the company will "make it up in volume". Well, the joke is on us. It is very difficult to "make it up in volume" when you cut prices. One of the first things that must be understood is that the amount of volume you need to "make up" for any given price cut is a function of your margins on what you sell.

GROSS MARGINS - WHO GETS WHAT?

The typical manufacturer's gross margin will run somewhere between 30% and 35%, the retailer will usually run 35% up to 40%, and the typical wholesaler's will run 25% to 35%. Therefore, most businesses realize gross margins on the products that they sell of about 25% to 40%. Some products run higher, and some run lower, but that range will put a bracket on the products of about 95% of the businesses in the United States[13]. Therefore, for our purposes here, I'm going to use a 35% gross margin. This is an average for most businesses and their products.

If you're interested in why some business gross margins are higher than others, the answer is fairly simple. Generally, *the easier it is to sell the product, the lower the gross margin.* This is because the people who enter those businesses usually don't know or care that much about selling . They just figure "I can sell that stuff." The trouble is that most people don't like to sell. Consequently more people enter these businesses, and because they tend to use low price as their sales tool, they bid down each other's prices to "hard to survive" levels. For example: more restaurants fail than jewelry stores. Everybody "knows", of course, that food is easier to sell than diamonds. Perhaps it's easier to sell food, but it seems like it is harder to profit from selling food. Selling skills always bring higher rewards to the people who can sell. Giving things away seldom rewards the giver, at least financially, which may account for the low pay of social workers.

NO PAIN, NO GAIN

Just because you are in a low margin business doesn't mean you can't make money. There have been large fortunes made in low margin businesses. But one truth does prevail. The lower the gross margin, the greater the pain, and the greater the gain, relative to cutting and/or raising prices in that business. For

---

13   Robert Morris Associates, *1991 Annual Statement Studies*, Philadelphia, PA, 1991.

example, when one cuts price 10% in a business that has products in the 35% gross margin range, they will probably only have to double the amount of product they sell at that price to "make it up in volume". But a business with a 25% margin, for the same 10% price cut, will probably have to sell more than three times as much volume to "make it up".

Conversely, when price is raised, the gain is greater in the lower margin business. For example, in a 35% gross margin business, when price is raised 10%, sales can fall about 34% and the company will make the same amount of money it was making before the price increase. But if a company with a 25% gross margin raises prices 10%, it can probably lose 41% or so of its business, and still make the same amount of money.

IF YOU CUT PRICE, YOU MUST SELL *HOW MUCH* MORE? HOGWASH!!

Many will, perhaps, say hogwash to the above suggestions that if you cut prices 10% on a 35% margin, you must sell nearly twice as much; if you raise prices 10%, you can lose 34% or so of your sales (and the corresponding quantities on 25% margins). Well, it's true. Let's look at why. Consider the following Profit and Loss statement on the widgets we are selling:

Figure 1

Sales	1,000,000	1.00%
COGS	650,000	.65
GM	350,000	.35
GSA/Fixed	200,000	
Variable	150,000	.15
	0	

.20 profit potential
on each one we sell
(.35 - .15 = .20)

Let's look at this company's figures. The Profit and Loss Statement above shows that we are selling $1,000,000 worth of these widgets and our cost of goods sold is

$650,000. That gives us a gross margin of $350,000.

What does gross margin mean? It means that when we sell something for a dollar, and it costs us 65¢ to have it to sell[14], you've got a 35¢ gross profit (or a 35% gross margin) on your sales dollar. What gross margin really means is that your gross profit potential on any given dollar of sales is only 35¢ because you've got to pay for what it is that you've sold.

From the gross margin one must subtract what are known as GS&A expenses (General, Selling and Administrative expenses). Some accountants call them SG&A (selling, general, administrative), while others call them Operating Expenses, but it all means the same thing. GS&A costs are the cost of administering the sales and administrative operations of the business, the cost of the office, the cost of the computer, telephone, desks and chairs, the cost of customer service. In short, the cost of the "head shed".

Of your GS&A expenses, some are fixed and some are variable. For example, in many businesses, office salaries are fixed. They don't have much to do with sales volume. Likewise, many other office costs are fixed: the cost of the computer, cost of occupying the offices, the heat, lights, utilities, insurance, etc. Those kinds of things are essentially the same from month to month, summer to winter, spring to fall. Other fixed costs are often budgeted costs and include such things as advertising and marketing costs. In our example, those costs run about $200,000.

The other GS&A costs are variable expenses. Variable GS&A expenses are those things that almost always vary with your sales volume. For example, when you sell something you've got to invoice for it. If you didn't sell it, you wouldn't have to go to that expense. When someone pays the invoice by sending you a check, you've got to process the check, etc. If you don't sell anything, you don't have these expenses; when you sell something, you do. In addition, there are many other kinds of GS&A costs that vary with your sales volume. For instance, you have to reorder things to replace what you've sold, or you won't have anything to sell in the future. Other variable GS&A expenses are credit and collections costs

---

14   If you're a manufacturer it costs you 65¢ to make it to sell, if you're a wholesaler, distributor, or retailer, it costs you 65¢ to buy it to have it to resell. You always subtract that 65¢ of what it costs you to have it to sell from your $1.00 of sales.

(the more you sell, the more credits and collection activity you must engage in) and customer service costs. In addition, commissions on sales are a variable expense. The point is, your variable expenses are expenses that essentially occur *because you sold something* and, the more you sell, the more of these costs you incur. Let's say your variable GS&A costs are running $150,000 and that means you're breaking even on the sale of this product.

As stated previously, business is really a game of margins, not volume. Here's why: After you have paid the costs that are directly incurred each and every time you sell something, you only have a few pennies (%, margin points) left from that sales dollar with which to try to earn a profit. This is because each time you sell another item of product, the direct costs are again incurred for the sale of that additional product, the same as those costs were incurred by each and every sale of each preceeding item. Therefore, looking at Figure 1, we can see that the Profit Potential on the sale of any given widget is 20¢ (obtained by subtracting the percentage of each sales dollar that goes for the cost of the product we sold and the cost of GS&A expenses directly attributable to that sale.) This Profit Potential is most easily gained by subtracting your variable GS&A expenses from your gross margin. For example, if your variable expenses are $150,000, they are 15% of your sales price. So really, when you sell something for $1.00, and you've got 65¢ cost of goods sold (which leaves us a 35% gross margin), we must still subtract our variable expense percent (15%) from that gross margin percent to determine what our true profit potential is on any given dollar of sale. But 20¢ is still only a *profit potential* as we still have not deducted our fixed costs.

In short, when we sell something for a buck, and we've paid all the costs of having it to sell and the direct costs associated with selling it, we've really only got a 20¢ profit potential on any given dollar of sales. And that 20¢ has to cover our fixed costs. Well, on $1,000,000 in sales, 20¢ on the dollar is $200,000, and our fixed costs are $200,000, so we break even at a million in sales. Up to the point of $1,000,000 in sales, all of our 20¢ potential profit on each sale must be used to cover our fixed costs. At $1,000,000 in sales, our fixed costs are perfectly covered; on any sales past $1,000,000 those 20¢ pieces of profit potential remain as profit for the company.

THE BREAK EVEN FORMULA

From the above analysis, we are now in a position to understand a formula that can be used to calculate a product's Break Even Volume. That is:

Break Even Volume = $\dfrac{\text{\$ Fixed GS\&A costs}}{\text{Gross Margin\% - Variable expense \%}}$

Your break even volume is equal to your dollars of fixed GS &A costs, divided by your gross margin percent, minus your variable expense percent.

Let's see how the formula works. As we look at our profit and loss statement in Figure 1, we see that fixed costs are $200,000 which is to be divided by our gross margin of 35% (.35 written as a decimal) minus our variable expense percent of 15% (.15 written as a decimal). That equals $200,000 divided by .20 (which is the profit potential that we have left when we subtract our variable expense percent from our gross margin). You can tell by looking at it (or by working the formula) that the answer then becomes $1,000,000. Figure 2 shows the calculations.

Figure 2

B/E Volume	=	$\dfrac{\$200,000}{.35 - .15}$
	=	$\dfrac{\$200,000}{.20}$
	=	$1,000,000

WHAT HAPPENS WHEN YOU CUT PRICE 10%

Now let's take a look at what you do to yourself when you cut the price of your product. If you cut your price 10% (let's assume that we sell the exact same amount of product -- no more, no less -- because then we can see precisely what happens to our margins as a consequence of that price cut) your revenues then would only be $900,000 (rather than $1,000,000) because you are getting only 90¢ for each one sold rather than $1.00 each. Your cost of goods sold, however, will still be the same $650,000 because you sold the exact same amount of product.

Your gross margin, therefore, becomes $250,000.

The rest of the statement stays the same, except for the fact that the company lost $100,000. (But that, of course, makes sense -- if you were doing $1 million in sales, were breaking even, and you cut your price 10% and sell the same amount, you are going to lose $100,000.) Figure 3 shows the results.

Figure 3

Sales	$900,000	100%
COGS	650,000	72.2%
GM	250,000	27.8%
GSA/	200,000	
Variable	150,000	16.7%
	(100,000)	11.1% PP

Now our cost of goods sold happens to be .722 percent of our selling price, and our gross margin happens to be .278. Notice, by cutting your price 10%, your gross margin falls from .35 to .278, which is better than a 20% drop in your gross margin. It is a .072 drop (from .35 to .278) as a percentage of *sales*, but a better than 20% drop as a percentage of the original gross margin of 35%. When you cut your price by 10% on a 35% gross margin, you cut your gross margin in excess of 20%:

$$(.35 - .278 = .072. \quad \frac{.072}{.35} = .2057 \text{ or } 20.57\%)$$

That's what happens to our gross margin -- but there's more bad news. We have to look at our GS & A expenses to see the total impact of our price cut. Our fixed expenses are still going to stay the same $200,000, and our variable expenses are going to stay the same $150,000. But your variable expense *percent* now has become .167 of your selling price. And our profit potential (the spread that we realize by subtracting our variable expense percent from our gross margin) is now $.111, when before it was 20¢. Translation: You cut your price 10% on a product with a 35% gross margin, you will cut your profit potential on each dollar of sales nearly in half, from 20¢ on each one you sell to 11.1¢.

Remember our formula? By doing the above, we now have the three numbers that we need to calculate our new break even volume. Figure 4 shows the results. Our $200,000 of fixed costs have stayed the same, but our gross margin has fallen from .35 to .278. Our variable expense percent has increased from .15 to .167, and the spread that we call profit potential, which was 20¢, is now only 11.1¢. Our new break even volume can then be calculated, which is $1,801,801.80.

Figure 4

$$\text{B/E Volume} = \frac{\$200,000}{.278 - .167}$$

$$= \frac{\$200,000}{.111}$$

$$= \$1,801,801.80$$

What that tells us is, if you cut your price 10% on a product with a 35% gross margin, you're going to have to increase your sales volume from $1,000,000 of that product to $1,801,801.80 *just to make the same amount of money you were making* (i.e., to get back to our break even volume). Figure 5 shows the calculation. By looking at Figure 5 you can see that, with sales of $1,801,801.80, our cost of goods sold is $1,300,900.80 (.722% of our selling price). Our gross margin, in dollars, is $500,901.00 (.278% of our sales). Of our GS&A expenses, our fixed expenses are $200,000 and our variable expenses are $300,900.76 (.167 of our sales). That leaves us with a 24¢ profit (because of rounding errors) but I think most readers would agree a 24¢ profit on $1,801,801.80 in sales is roughly break even.

Figure 5

Sales	$1,801,801.80	100%
COGS	1,300,900.80	72.2%
GM	500,901.00	27.8%
GSA/fixed	200,000.00	
/variable	300,900.76	16.7%
	.24	

What all of this means is if you cut your price 10% on a 35% gross margin item, your sales volume has to increase from $1,000,000 to $1,801,801.80 which is an 80% increase in *dollar* sales, but a *doubling* in the quantity of product that you must sell. In fact, it is a little more than double. Why double and not 80%? Because you must sell $1,801,801.80 in sales dollars, but you are only getting 90¢ for each unit you sell. $1,800,000, at 90¢ each is twice as many units of product sold as $1,000,000 at $1 each. (It is also evident that we must double our sales when we look at our cost of goods sold which has had to increase from $650,000 to $1,300,900.80; that is more than a 100% increase in the number of units of product that must be sold at cost). Translation: On a typical business gross margin of about 35% on a product, if you cut your price 10%, you have to sell about twice as much. And that still isn't all the bad news. The lower your margin, the worse it gets. If the gross margin on your product is down around 25%, you will have to sell over 3 times as much product to make up for the same 10% price cut.

IMPLICATIONS FOR THE REAL WORLD

Let's consider a couple of real world implications of the foregoing:

Question #1. If you cut your price 10%, do you think you'd sell twice as much volume in units?

Answer: Probably not, especially if your competition follows by cutting their price, too. Truth is, you probably wouldn't sell a lot more and nowhere near twice as much.

Question #2. If you cut your price 10% and you get the orders for twice as much product, *can you ship it? On time?*

Answer: Probably not. If you've got to ship twice as much product in the same amount of time, then your business had better be running at *less than half its capacity*, or otherwise you're going to be in the ignominious situation of having cut price and taken orders for product that you can't ship on time. And remember, your business must be running at less than 50% of your capacity across the board, in every dimension of the business -- plant, office, warehouse, number of employees available, ability to carry twice the inventory, accounts receivable, storage capacity, distribution, filing, data processing, telephone calls, customer service, etc., etc. If your business isn't at less than 50% of capacity in *all affected dimensions*, it will be physically impossible to ship to your customer on time, whether you get the orders or not.

Those of you who are manufacturers, before you ever consider cutting price, had better think long and hard about this question: Can we *make* it and *ship* it on time, even if we get the orders? And for those of you who are wholesalers and distributors and retailers, don't just think, "Well, hell, we'll just order more." You better give serious thought to this question: Can your manufacturers and suppliers ship to you -- on time? And *will* they ship to you? Will they be willing to double your credit line? Do they have the capacity to ship to you? Maybe they do, but I bet every one of you have had the experience where they said, "We'll have to put you on back order. We might be able to ship that to you in 4 months." It's tough to cut price -- and make it up in volume. Especially if you really *get* the orders.

Question #3. If we do cut price 10%, and we get the necessary quantity of orders to "make it up in volume", and we can ship it on time, who are we going to get for new customers?

Answer: Price-buyers. Chiselers. Slow-payers.

Question #4. If we can accomplish the foregoing, and are willing to put up with an increased number of price-buyers among our customers, are we really willing to do all that extra work, *and* not earn any more money for the company?

Answer: That's right. You pull off all the above and you are only back to where you were breaking even on the sale of this product. Doesn't seem like a very intelligent decision to choose to work harder for the same amount of profit.

CHAPTER 9

YEAH, BUT I'LL MAKE MORE $
IF I CUT MY PRICE --
AND I DON'T CARE IF
MY COMPANY DOES GO BROKE

"I was looking for a job when I got
this one."
Anonymous

Many sales people will read the foregoing chapter and think, "Okay, so the company won't make any more money if I cut my price. But I will. And (honestly) I don't care if the company goes broke. After all, I was looking for a job when I got this one. I'll just go sell for someone else." Well, let's take a look at that idea.

WHAT HAPPENS IF WE RAISE PRICE?

What happens if we raise price? You can lose a lot of volume -- maybe a third of your volume (on a 35% gross margin and 10% price increase) or more (41% of your volume on a 25% gross margin for the same price increase) and still make as much money. Let's work the numbers out because this knowledge is what gives sales people real backbone in facing down those purchasing agents, buyers and customers that want to hammer you on price.

Figure 6

Sales	**$1,100,000**	**100%**
COGS	**650,000**	**59%**
GM	**450,000**	**41%**
GSA/Fixed	**200,000**	
/variable	**150,000**	**13.6%**
	$ 100,000	**27.4% profit potential**

In Figure 6 it can be seen that if we raise price 10% (and we assume that we sell the same amount of volume in order to determine the impact of our price increase on our margins) our sales revenues will be $1,100,000. We're selling the same amount, but we're selling it at $1.10. Our cost of goods sold, however, will remain the same $650,000 because we sold the same amount and it will therefore cost the same. Our gross margin now will be $450,000. With our higher price, now our cost of goods sold is 59% of our selling price and our gross margin is 41%. Notice, by raising our price 10%, our gross margin increases from .35 to .41 (which is about a 17% increase in our gross margin). Our fixed expenses are still going to be the same $200,000 that they were, our variable expenses essentially will stay the same $150,000 that they were, and now we're going to make $100,000 in profit.

But the increase in profit is not what we're concerned with at this point. What I'm trying to show here is what happens to your margins as a consequence of your price increase. Now your variable expense percent is .136 of your selling price and, remember, our profit potential on a given dollar of sales is that spread that we get when we subtract our variable expense percent from our gross margin. The profit potential on each one sold was 20¢, now it is $.274.   By raising our price 10%, we increase our profit potential on any given dollar of sales 37%. Again, no magic act, that's just the way it is. And, again, by doing this we have the margins that we need to use in our formula to determine how much volume we need to sell at these margins to break even. That will then tell us how much sales volume we can *lose* as a result of our higher price and still make as much money as we were making. Figure 7 shows those calculations.

Figure 7

$$\text{B/E Volume} = \frac{\text{\$ Fixed GSA Costs}}{\text{Gross Margin \% - Variable Expense \%}}$$

$$= \frac{\$200,000}{.41 - .136}$$

$$= \frac{\$200,000}{.274}$$

$$= \$729,927.00$$

By using our formula we can determine that the volume required as a consequence of our higher price is only $729,927.

Figure 8 shows the verification of this. There it can be seen that if you multiply $729,927 by 59% (which is the percentage that our cost of goods sold is of our new, higher sales price), you'll find that your cost of goods sold in dollars will be $430,656.93. Subtracting (or multiplying your sales by 41% which is your gross margin) shows that your gross profit is $299,270.07. The fixed GS&A costs are the same $200,000, and we can find our variable expenses by multiplying sales by .136 (which is our variable expense percent). Our variable expenses are, therefore, $99,270.07 and that comes to a perfect zero or break even (not even any rounding error problem).

Figure 8

Sales	$729,927.00	100%
COGS	430,656.93	59%
GM	299,270.07	41%
GSA/Fixed	200,000.00	
/Variable	99,270.07	13.6
	0.00	

This shows that by raising our price 10% on these widgets, our sales could fall from $1,000,000 (where we started before we raised price) to $729,927 which is a 27% decline in our dollar sales. But remember, those are in $1.10 dollars-per-unit because of our new, higher price. It's our cost of goods sold that will tell us how many *units* of sales that we can lose in sales volume, and that has fallen from $650,000 to $430,656.93 . That represents just at a 34% decline in the number of units that one needs to sell at the higher price for the company *to make the same amount of money it was making*. In short, if you raise your price 10% on a 35% gross margin product, you can lose roughly a little more than a third of all the sales you've been making and make the same amount of money.

YEAH, BUT I'M NOT GOING TO MAKE AS MUCH

Let's face some reality here. Right now some of you (especially those paid on commission) have ambivalent feelings about the above. It isn't the math that's bothering you. You understand that. But your ambivalence goes back to the "something beats nothing all to hell" trick. You are thinking: If I raise price and lose volume, *I'm* going to lose money because I'm paid commission on sales, and that will hurt in *my* checkbook. If I raise price and lose a third of my sales, my commission isn't going to go down by 33%, but it's going to go down.

Don't worry about that. Here's why: (A) It's doubtful that your sales will fall that much. Sure, they could; but most times they don't and, often, they don't fall *at all*. They may even go up (price makes a statement -- a positive, salutory statement). (B) Your ability to provide *better*, more *timely* delivery of *quality* product, backed up by *superb* service to your customer will definitely improve when (if) you do lose a little volume. This tends to assure continued, profitable sales to your non-price buying customers. (C) The company almost assuredly will start making more money (unless total sales do fall by *more* than 33%) which means that you'll find bonus money in your paycheck and/or improving commission rates. This is especially true if your bonus is tied to company profits, and/or your commission *rate* goes up as your sales price goes up, and/or if your commission is dependent upon your company's gross profit percentage. In short, you are worth more as a sales rep because the company is making more. They won't want to lose you and they are fools not to reward you. Good, profitable sales reps are hard to come by and are always well paid, in contrast to order takers who give away product.

WHY GO BROKE TIRED?

Two things sales reps who sell at high prices learn early is that (A) if you sell at a low price, your company is going to cut your comission rate (because they have to when they start losing money) and (B) if you sell at a low price, you are necessarily going to inflict an *incredible* amount of work *on yourself* to try to maintain those (paltry) commissions. Here's why: Let's say you are selling $1,000,000 of this product yourself ($650,000 at cost of goods sold). If you (and your company) *raise* price 10%, you have to sell only $430,656.93 (in cost of goods sold) of this product. *Cost of goods sold* tells us the number of *units* of product we must sell because it puts a dollar value on the number of units you must sell at your higher price to get back to where the company is breaking even. Cost of goods sold is a way of putting a dollar value on how much work you (and your company) must do -- how many orders the company has to get, produce, fill, ship and deliver on time. But the sales rep who cuts price by 10% has to sell, in terms of cost of goods sold, $1,300,900.83. That means that the guy who cuts his price has to sell *three times* as much product in units to enable the company to make the same amount of money it would make by the rep selling at the high price. *If you're going to go broke, why go broke tired?* If you are going to have to find another job because your company went broke, why do so much churning? If you (or your company) are going to go broke because of a pricing error, you always want to go broke *over*pricing. Any idiot can cut price, get volume, go broke and grow tired. If you're going to make a mistake in pricing, you always want to make the mistake on the high side. It doesn't take near the work to go broke overpricing that it does to go broke underpricing.

NOBODY CAN MAKE ANY MONEY WORKING AT EL CHEAPOS.

It's amazing to me the number of people who see volume and confuse it with prosperity and success -- particularly when they see the volume being done at El Cheapos. Volume just creates a lot of hard work -- not profit.

When you're working for El Cheapos, they probably are not paying you very much money, let alone giving you any kinds of perks and benefits. For example,

87

many people thought that People Express Airlines was a very successful airline -- look at the volume they did. But certainly the people that worked at People Express didn't make much money; and they were pressured into buying stock in lieu of taking their earnings in wages. Then when the company went belly up, who do you think the losers were? Who do you actually think paid for those cheap airplane seats in which everybody was flying around? The employees, of course.

Donald Burr, the founder and Chief Executive Officer of People Express Airlines, pretty well put his finger on some of the absurdities of figuring that anybody working at a high-volume, low-price business is likely to have a highly rewarding financial career. For example, he was quoted in *Inc.* magazine[15] as follows: "I knew I was in trouble when my mother was coming up to visit me and she said, 'I hope you don't mind, but I'm flying American. Just a few dollars more.' "

One must certainly wonder why "Mommy" preferred to fly American Airlines -- and pay a little more money. It seems likely that American Airlines was perceived as a better deal to her than People Express. And one must certainly wonder why "Mommy" even had to pay for her own airplane ticket, particularly when she was the mother of the President, founder, Chairman of the Board, and major shareholder of People Express Airlines? Would you have made your mommy pay for her own airline ticket on your airline?

It's truly interesting when one looks very closely at the welfare of employees who work for discounting operations. Ultimately, they never make any real money -- because the company never makes any real money.

WE WERE BUSY RIGHT UP TO THE LAST DAY

The other day I got off an airplane in Indianapolis, Indiana. The flight crew that flew my plane was riding on the courtesy bus with me over to the hotel. A couple of the stewardesses were just talking, apparently about a retail store. One of them says, "Hey, I hear that old Schwartzheimer's is going out-of-business."

---

15   *Inc.* , April 1987, p. 23.

The other one says, "Oh, no. You're kidding. That's my favorite store. Why?"

First one says, "Gee, I don't know. Somebody said they weren't making any money."

Other one says, "Oh, can't be. Every time I've been in there, they have just been jammed full of customers."

I felt like saying, "Let me get my Break Even Formula out and explain it to you. I think I can explain why they were busy right up to the last day -- but the employees didn't make any money and the company went broke."

You've probably heard someone talking about having gone bust in a business. Almost always, if you ask them what happened they will scratch their head and say, "Gee, I don't know. You know, we were busy right up to the last day." Remember what we said at the beginning of this book? When businesses go bust, they virtually always do so during a period of sales volume increase because they have cut their price. When they cut their price, their gross margin goes down and their sales go up. But if sales don't go up enough, the company goes broke.

Have you ever worked for an unprofitable business? If you have, you probably learned that it's not any fun. I have a little sign in my office that says, "It isn't fun if it isn't profitable". If you have worked for both profitable and unprofitable businesses, I think you would agree, it's more fun when the company is making money. I have never heard anybody complain about excessive frugality in successful businesses; but I sure have heard about "the need to tighten up" in an unprofitable business.

I *STILL* SAY I'D MAKE MORE MONEY
SELLING AT THE LOWER PRICE

"Okay, okay," you say. "I understand that when companies are operating on slim margins that everything has to be tight. But I could sell more at a lower price and, consequently, *I'd* make more money even if (or until) the company goes broke." Even if the company lets you cut your price and you sell more, it is unlikely that you'd actually make more money. Here's why:

Let's say you personally have been selling a million dollars worth of this product. And let's say that your commission is 7% on sales. That gives you a $70,000 commission income. Obviously, if your company would let you cut the price by 10% *and you could double your sales*, your sales volume would go to $1,800,000 (in dollars) and you, of course, would receive 7% of the $1,800,000, so your commission income would rise from $70,000 a year to $126,000. Certainly you'd be better off, right?

Maybe you'd be better off, but consider this: You'd be making $126,000, which would represent an 80% increase in your commission income. But *you'd have to be selling twice as much product* and, in all likelihood, your competition would counter with another price cut *which would put you back on a level playing field.*

The point is this: competition does not fail to react. You start cutting the price 10%, and you can pretty well bet your competition will, too. That puts you back at the same relative price as your competitor. When that happens what are the probabilities that you'll actually sell a significant *additional* amount of volume, let alone twice as much? Once you're back on a level playing field, the only additional increase in sales volume that you will realize will occur from customers who have not been buying the product to begin with (the incremental customer for your product)   or the customer who will buy a little more of your product (the one who thinks not only your product, but everybody else's that you compete with has been priced too high in the past).   The probability of a significant increase in sales volume for your firm from these sources, I feel, is very small -- because your competitors will get their share, too.

Furthermore, once back on a level playing field, you're going to have to sell *twice* as much product. But even if you do that, you're only going to make *80%* more. That means that you're going to work twice as hard to make 80% more. If you're really willing to work twice as hard to make 80% more money, why don't you work twice as hard on the deal you already have? Why don't you go out right now and work *twice* as hard and make *twice* as much?

90

It's amazing to me the number of sales reps that don't clearly understand the foregoing logic. Over and beyond that, it is even more amazing to me the number of sales reps that fail to understand what is likely to happen if your company does cut the price so that they can sell more.

If you're paid commission, there's an incredibly high probability that when your company cuts price, they're going to cut your commission *rate*. The reason they have to do that is they cannot afford to pay you as high a commission rate when you are selling (giving away?) product at a lower price. Like we said before: if we want someone to give away our product, we can go over to the welfare department and hire social workers.

My personal studies show that when the typical sales rep, who's receiving a 7% commission rate, cuts their price by 10%, he/she will probably experience about a 40% cut in their commission rate (40% of 7% is .028%. You subtract .028% from .07% and that will leave you with .042%.) Now consider this. You cut your price 10% and your sales volume increases from $1,000,000 to $1,800,000; but they cut your commission rate from .07% to .042%. You'll find that .042% of $1,800,000 happens to be $75,600. That means that if you go out and sell twice as much product at your new lower price (in the face of your competitors having lowered their price) your commission income will increase "dramatically" from $70,000 to $75,600 -- or an 8% increase. Now, how many of you really want to sell twice as much product to make 8% more -- whether the company goes broke or not!

The long and the short of this whole section is that if you cut your price, you're probably not going to make significantly more money -- you are just going to work harder. And the reason you're not going to make significantly more money is because your company *can't afford to pay you any more money.*

Conversely, don't ever feel that if you raise your price, you are not going to make as much money. I guarantee you that if you sell at a good high price and keep your company profitable, you're going to make a lot more money. Companies want to keep *profitable* sales reps on the payroll, and they pay them big bucks. Companies can't afford to pay big bucks to people who are giving things away. This is why today many businesses are compensating sales people not on the volume of sales they obtain, but against *gross margin* or *profitability* on those sales. They do this because they have to if they are going to remain in business.

OUR NATIONAL CASE STUDY IN PRICING STRATEGIES
(OR LET'S EVERYBODY CUT PRICE AND
WE'LL ALL MAKE IT UP IN VOLUME)

As the first part of this chapter shows, it is very difficult to cut price and make it up in volume. Yet it seems that the woods are full of people (business people -- even highly educated business people) who don't (or *won't*) understand bankruptcy. The airlines are a good example, and airline deregulation is a good case in point about the typical business person's propensity to cut price in the blind belief that "we can make it up in volume."

In 1978, President Jimmy Carter deregulated the airlines. This meant that, overnight, the U.S. airlines were free to charge any price they wanted. How many raised price? None that I know of. And, as pointed out in Chapter 1, the number of airlines filing for bankruptcy since airline deregulation (as of the time of this writing) is close to 300.

The behavior of the business people running U.S. airlines subsequent to deregulation proved that there is a latent bias upon the part of most people in business to cut price. The moment they were free to charge any price they wanted, they all started cutting their prices.

Where does this bias come from? It probably will be a surprise to you, but I'd like to share this thought that someone gave me a few years ago: Most of us learn that "you can cut your price and make it up in volume" in Econ 101, because that is where most of the preachments about cutting price and making it up in volume originate. Did it ever occur to you (prior to just now) that the professor of economics that taught you Econ 101, who was making $27,000 a year, had a latent bias against high prices? Did you ever think that, perhaps, this (often) liberal professor of economics, making $27,000 a year, who taught you Econ 101, had a latent desire to get you capitalist pigs to go out in the business world and *give away your products so his $27,000 a year would go further?*

If you are ever going to make your prices stick, you must understand the economics of pricing. Understanding the volumes required to "make up" for a price cut can instill in you a lot of courage against cutting your prices. Don't ever forget the break even formula. It will make you a ton of money because it will break you of that idea that you can cut price and make it up in volume. If you want to earn a living selling, you must remember that you are going to have a perennial challenge to your ability (and desire) to hang on to a high price because you will always have to compete with some idiot who is going broke cutting prices. That's never going to go away. And, worse yet, when that somebody goes broke, someone else is going to come crawling out of the woodwork, thinking they are a "little smarter than the average bear", and that, "these guys that are in the business are charging too much", and that, "we can cut the price, make it up in volume, and make more money."

Remember, there have been nearly 300 airlines that have gone bust since deregulation, and there have been 215 new airlines *started* since deregulation. I'll guarantee you that many of them have thought, "Well, I'm smarter than those idiots that are running those airlines. I can sell at a lower price and we'll make it up in volume because I took Econ 101." You're going to be hammered forever by price-cutting fools. Just accept that. But, ultimately, if your price is to be cut, *YOU* will be the one who will cut *YOUR* price. And you'll do that because you don't know how to sell quality, service and delivery.

CHAPTER 10

HOW TO FACE A COMPETITOR'S PRICE CUTS

"When you are in a price war, you
learn to stay low."
Billboard ad of defunct
automobile dealer in Michigan

There are many things that you might do when you're faced with a cut in price by a competitor. Let's consider some of the situations that may prevail and what you might do about them.

Situation 1. You don't know for sure, whether your competitor has cut your price or by how much.

Solution: Hold your price at the present level and watch your competitor, particularly your competitor's volume of shipments and receipt of materials. If you just "hear tell" that your competition is offering their product at a lower price, try to determine if they really are offering that price. When your customer says "I can get it cheaper down the street", you have to try to verify that. That's called doing your homework. In the military service we called it "G2" -- intelligence.

I don't want to suggest that you do anything illegal, immoral or unethical, but I will advocate that you learn to do a little legal spying. Is your competition *really* offering that lower price, or are they only offering that lower price when they can't ship it? Or is there some other catch -- like, yes, the price is being offered, but only if you buy the purple ones with green and burnt-orange polka dots; or only if you buy a 92-year supply; or only if you agree *not* to buy from someone else for 46 years; or some other ridiculous, essentially unrealistic "requirement". Do some verification. And even if you determine they *are* offering that price, you still need to determine two more things: Are your customers buying at that price? And is your competitor, who is offering that price, both *shipping and receiving?* If customers are buying, and your competition is both shipping at that lower price and receiving, that says one thing. However, if they are shipping but not receiving, you can probably bet that they are dropping the line or they're going out-of-business.

Your first determination must be: Are they charging that price, getting orders *and* shipping and receiving at that price? If they aren't shipping, forget about it. No reason to cut your price. If they're charging that price and they're shipping but they're not receiving, still there's no reason to cut the price. They're soon going to run out of that product and aren't going to have any more to sell.

Many sales reps, of course, ask, "How do I know if they're shipping and receiving?" It's simple. Do a little homework. Call them and ask them (you'd be surprised what motor-mouthed employees will tell anonymous telephone callers). Or drive by their place and give it a "windshield appraisal". Often you can tell how busy a place is by their inventory stored outside, the number of cars in the employee parking lot or the number of cars in the customer lot. Or you can tell whether a business is busy just by driving around the block at quitting time, or by assessing how much smoke's coming out of the chimney, how many people are walking around, how many trucks are backed up at the loading docks. Walk through their store if you are a retailer. The things you can do are only limited by your imagination.

Another thing you can do is check the local bar (where your competitor's employees go after work). You'd be amazed what you can learn. Ask questions like, "How's business?" "You hiring anybody?" "How's that promotion going on X product, etc., etc., etc?" If the competition knows your face, you can always send someone else in to ask the questions for you.

There are a multiplicity of other ways to get information about whether or not your competitor is (A) getting orders, (B) at that price, and (C) shipping and receiving. So Situation #1 is simple. If you don't know whether your competition has cut their price, find out. And even if they have cut the price, find out if they are both shipping and receiving. Don't do *anything* to your price until you ascertain that all of the foregoing is happening.

Situation 2: Prices have been cut, for sure, but your volume is not being affected. Your sales are hanging in there, but they've cut their price.

Solution: Hold your price level until your competitor's price cut begins to significantly affect your volume. Maybe your competitor is at or near capacity and can't supply anymore. If your competitor is selling at that price, and he's shipping and receiving, but your volume's holding, your competitor is probably at or near capacity and he can't ship anymore. Look what happened to the airlines with People Express. Many airline companies said, "Hey, People Express is knocking the living daylights out of us. We have to do something; they're cutting our price." But the smarter companies simply said, "Let them fill up their airplanes and we'll fly the others. They don't have many airplanes. They are all flying full, and it doesn't look like they can get many more planes because nobody will sell (or lease) to them because they are having trouble paying their bills."

Brother & Sister

It's this simple. An airplane is only so big and it can only fly so fast. So why cut your price if your competitor is at or near capacity? Even if "everybody" is calling up and saying they can get it cheaper (fly cheaper) at People Express. Tell them to go fly on it -- if they can get a seat -- and they think it will leave on time so they can make their connection. Don't ever forget this. Virtually all businesses are capacity limited. And discounters almost always end up with delivery problems that quickly convert into quality problems, that rapidly become customer service problems, that cause customers to look for other vendors. At the end, most business travelers would have preferred to take a beating than have to fly on People Express. And who "supports" the airlines? Answer: business travelers.

Situation 3: Price has been cut, for sure, and your volume is being affected heavily. All right, now we're getting hurt on volume.

Solution: Hold your price and consider whether you might be able to stem your volume loss with extra advertising -- or by way of better service or package dealing. Especially consider how much your product (and company) image will be damaged by a price cut by you. Look at it like this. If you cut your price, you've got to get an incredible increase in volume (as per the foregoing mathematics of pricing). Secondly, if you cut price, you're probably going to hurt the image of your product. Third, it is mathematically true that, virtually always, if you will spend time and effort and money trying to make sure that you are giving your customer the quality, the service, and the delivery you've promised them, they won't go looking for other vendors. Spending money on correct quality, flawless service, and perfect delivery is virtually always less painful than if you cut your price. Just by way of example, for most businesses (assuming a 35% gross margin) if they triple their budget for customer service it will only take about a 5% increase in sales volume to make up for that effort. But if that business cuts it's price just 2% they will have to do 10 to 15% more in volume just to make up for that 2% price cut.[16]

As I previously mentioned, typically, those companies that have survived the longest have charged the highest prices and made the most money. And,

---

16   See Appendix One, p. 100 , for the mathematics of this.

invariably, they have competed on delivery, quality, and service. They know that if you cut your price, you plug up your business with unprofitable volume. And when you start having delivery, then quality, then service problems, you drive off your profitable customers.

The customer that a business gains because of low price is invariably the one that creates problems and destroys your ability to really sell to a profitable (i.e. nonprice-buying) customer. You've got to be willing to say to a price-buyer (who is, after all, devoted to the proposition that "you shan't make money on me") that, "I don't need your business. I can't afford to do business with you."

Situation 4: You're getting your pants beat off; cutting price is the only thing you can do; the writing's on the wall; there's no place to go.

Solution: O.K. I don't have answers for everything. It can get so bad, there is nothing else you can do but cut price. *But* if you must cut price, consider the following: (A) Run a temporary deal (if you can survive) to meet your competitor's price -- but it better be *temporary*. (B) Meet your competition if the cut is to be 10% or less on a short-term basis. But, again, remember a 10% cut on a typical gross margin of 35% means that you'll have to double the amount of work you're going to do, the product you have to sell, the effort you'll have to expend, just to stay "even on the boards". (C) Cut the line if the competitor's cut is to be permanent. If it's your only product, try to continue providing good quality, service and delivery and hope you can last longer than the competition.

At some point, obviously, there is no answer. If your competitor has a ton of money to lose (and substantially more to lose than you do) get the hell out. You will go broke before he does. But if you study the above, you will see that outside of competing with a kamikaze, there is no reason to be stampeded into taking a price cut to maintain business viability. Most price cutting is a *self-inflicted* wound because the people who do it don't understand anything other than selling on price. If you will learn to sell products and services on quality, service and delivery, and not on price, you'll find your business more profitable and your commission checks larger and more fulfilling.

You must recognize what you do to yourself and your company when you cut price. To be comfortable in avoiding price cutting, you must know what you're doing. That means study, education and thinking. A lot of people say study, education and thinking takes time and is very expensive. Well, if you think study, education and thinking is expensive, why don't you try ignorance.

APPENDIX ONE - CHAPTER 10

WHY IT IS ALMOST ALWAYS MORE SENSIBLE TO INCREASE YOUR ACTIVITIES IN THE AREA OF IMPROVING QUALITY, INCREASING YOUR EFFORTS IN CUSTOMER SERVICE, SPENDING MORE TIME ON ADVERTISING AND PROMOTION, AND INSURING THAT YOUR DELIVERY IS ON TIME, RATHER THAN CUTTING PRICE

It was stated in Chapter 10 that for most businesses, (assuming a 35% gross margin on what they're selling), if they triple their budget for customer service, it will only take about a 5% increase in sales volume to make up for that extra effort in customer service. Conversely, if they cut their price by just 2%, they will have to realize an increase in sales volume somewhere in the neighborhood of 10-15% just to make up for that 2% price cut.

For those readers who are interested in the mathematics of this, it can be ascertained as follows:

Let's say your business is doing about $1,000,000 in sales, and is paying somewhere in the neighborhood of $5,000 for customer service activity. That would mean that your company is spending approximately one-half of 1% of all sales dollars strictly for customer service.

Now, let's assume that your company decided to triple the amount of money they were spending on customer service, from $5,000 to $15,000, which would be an increase from one-half of 1% of sales to 1.5% of sales.

That increase in customer service would represent a $10,000 increase in GS & A expenses. We can consider that $10,000 increase as a sunk cost or a "fixed" cost.

The way to analyze the impact of this sunk cost in our break-even formula, of course, is to add the $10,000 in as an additional fixed cost. Our break-even formula originally was as follows:

$$\text{Break even volume} = \frac{\$200,000}{.35 - .15} = \frac{\$200,000}{.20} = \$1,000,000$$

If we increase our fixed overhead costs by $10,000, our formula would then be:

$$\frac{\$210,000}{.35 - .15} = \frac{\$210,000}{.20} = \$1,050,000$$

or a 5% increase in sales required to make up for that tripling of the amount of money which we spend on customer service. (Note both our sales *dollars* and sales *units* would only raise 5% because, by not having cut our price, our sales in units increase at exactly the same rate as our increase in sales dollars.)

What would happen if, rather than tripling the amount of time and effort that we spend on customer service, we decided to cut our price by 2%? That, too, can be considered by taking a look at our break-even formula.

If we cut our price by 2%, our break-even formula will be as follows:

$$\frac{\$200,000}{.3367 - .1531} = \frac{\$200,000}{.1836} = \$1,089,324$$

These are the numbers that would occur because of our price cut and its impact on our gross margin percentages and variable expense percentages. So that means that by cutting our price 2%, our sales dollars must increase by $89,324.

That is our dollar increase in sales. What tells us how many units of products we must sell? This can only be determined by converting our dollar sales into unit sales. That can be realized by multiplying our dollar sales by our cost of goods sold, which will have increased from .65 of our selling price to .6633 (because of our 2% price cut). If we multiply $1,089,324 by .6633, it tells us that our sales volume in units will be $722,549. This means an 11.16% increase in our sales volume will be required to make up for that 2% price cut.

A simple question is this: why is it that everybody wants to cut their price, with the bright idea they can make it up in volume? The facts are that if one will spend more money on quality, service and delivery, and/or devote more time to genuine customer service and/or devote more attention to detail, helping their customer, and otherwise generally doing the job right, it is almost always less painful than it is to try to cut price and make it up in volume.

CHAPTER 11

INDICATORS OF
UNDERPRICING

*"Nobody goes to Toots Shores
anymore - it's too crowded."*
Attributed to Yogi Berra

Baseball players say interesting things -- or, at least, interesting lines are attributed to them. One of Yogi Berra's most famous lines is: "It ain't over till it's over." You always hear that from the losers on election evening. Joe Garagiola isn't too bad, either. Of course, Joe and Yogi grew up together in St. Louis and were childhood playmates before they became major league catchers. Joe's famous one is, "Nolan Ryan is a much better pitcher now that he's got his curve ball straightened out." But Yogi game back with a couple other of my personal favorites which are: "If people don't want to come out to the ball game and watch it, I can't stop them." and, "Much can be observed by just watching."

IF PEOPLE DON'T WANT TO COME OUT TO THE BALL GAME
AND WATCH IT, I CAN'T STOP THEM

Much of the need for the material in this book is based on the insights of those last two statements. Many sales reps think the statement: "If people don't want to come out to the ball game and watch it, I can't stop them." is silly. Yet many a sales rep has told a sales manager, "If people don't want to buy our product, I can't stop them," (or something to that effect). Well, you sure *can* stop them if you learn to sell -- in contrast to taking orders. Selling is about getting somebody to buy something they might not otherwise buy because they lack knowledge or information. Many sales reps say they feel their customers don't buy because their products or services are too high priced when, in reality, they haven't learned to explain to their prospective customers why buying their product at a fair (high) price is going to be beneficial to them.

MUCH CAN BE OBSERVED BY JUST WATCHING

The intellectual treasure, "Much can be observed by just watching," runs in the same vein as the, "I can't make them buy it." line. There is a lot of truth in the statement that you can see a lot -- if you'll just look. And one of the things you can see is that your customers will alert you to when you can charge higher prices because they will tell you when your prices are too low. They will tell you, accurately and honestly, if you will just watch. They will tell you in the way they behave, the things they say and the things that they do. But you have to be watching in order to pick up on them.

When was the last time you worried that your prices were TOO LOW? If you are a typical sales rep -- and especially if you are a sales rep who is paid commission on the dollar volume you sell, the answer is PROBABLY NEVER. Very few sales reps ever worry that their prices are too low. They are so afraid of overpricing that they virtually never even imagine that their prices could be too low *and they virtually always end up underpricing because of it.*

I once met a contractor who specialized in installing railings on balconies in high-rise buildings. I asked him about his product liability problems, wondering about people falling over or through such railings. He stunned me with his answer which was: "What problems? Nobody ever tests the strength of those railings. They are so afraid of going over the edge that the most they'll do is stand two feet away and give them a little shake with their extended hand. The only reason a railing has to be strong is to withstand high winds. People will never deliberately test how strong a balcony railing is with their body."

The same thing holds true for testing prices. Virtually nobody will ever test to see if their price is high enough, always being afraid of going over the edge. It is for that reason that I am not nearly so concerned about indicators of prices being too high (although it is possible for prices to be too high and I've listed those indicators in Chapter 12). The latent propensity in most sales people in our society is to charge too low a price, as evidenced by the behavior of airlines when it came to deregulation.

IF YOU EVER MAKE A PRICING ERROR, YOU SHOULD MAKE IT ON THE HIGH SIDE

If you ever want to sell at a high price, you'll learn that you always want to make any mistake in your price on the high side. There are several reasons for this. Reason number one is that if your price is too high, it's always easier to lower your price than to raise your price. Reason number two is that if your prices are too low, it is tough to raise prices -- people almost always will resist a price increase, even when warranted, wanting to know why and how you can justify it; but they will respond warmly to a price decrease. Reason number three is that overpricing isn't nearly as hazardous to your business health as is underpricing. As we pointed out in the section on volume swings in Chapter 8, one can work their buns off and go broke underpricing. But if you go broke overpricing, you don't have to work as hard. You're not going to be any less broke if you go broke overpricing, but you won't be as tired. And, frankly, if you are a business owner, your business probably won't die any faster if you are going broke overpricing. Fact is, most businesses can survive a lot longer with *no* business volume than they can with *unprofitable* business volume. With the understanding that if you are going to make an error, it is more logical to overprice, let's think about what the indicators are that your price might be too low.

- *YOUR GROSS MARGIN IS GETTING SMALLER ON THE SAME OR RISING SALES VOLUME.*

If your gross profit margin begins to decline, especially on rising sales volume, you probably have too low a price. (Incidentally, the reverse of that is also true. If your gross margin begins to climb on decreasing sales, your prices are probably too high.) If you want to talk about how to fine tune to the right price, start by monitoring your gross margin *by product line.* For those of you who have only one product line, that's great; but wholesalers, distributors, and retailers who have thousands of line items aren't going to like this advice.

However, it is the only way to determine the right price and, with the use of a computer, it isn't that hard to do. Learn to use a computer for what it is designed to do -- crunch numbers.

If you want to be successful and sell at a high price, that feat will not occur as a result of a series of propitious accidents. Being successful is a function of knowing what you're doing, and that does take effort -- effective effort. Everybody I know who is in a highly profitable business carefully monitors gross margins. If you don't feel like doing it yourself, or if you say you don't have time, you had better learn to delegate because without that knowledge you are powerless to determine a rational pricing strategy.

- *YOUR NET PROFIT IS GOING DOWN.*

Net profit decline is not *necessarily* a sign that prices are too low, but it *may* be a flag to that effect. If your gross margin is also going down while your sales are going up, you have a pretty serious indication that your prices are too low. Again, I can't over-emphasize how important gross margin is in determining if your prices are too low -- or too high. You should price to achieve a constant, profitable gross margin on increasing sales brought about by selling good quality with impeccable service and, of course, on-time delivery.

- *PRICES ARE BELOW YOUR COMPETITORS.*

If your prices are below your competitors (unless that is your deliberate, conscious intention) your prices are probably too low. Remember price makes a statement -- a statement about not only the *quality* of your product, but the *advisability* of doing business with you. As I said in Chapter 3, if you were offered a new Rolls Royce for $47,000, you'd ask what's wrong with it, or do you have title to it? You'd think that it was somehow damaged or stolen. If you tell someone your product is cheaper, they'll believe you, in every sense of the word. Low price makes a statement: a diminutive statement. High price also makes a statement: a positive, salutory statement.

- *THERE IS A LOT OF TALK BY YOUR CUSTOMERS ABOUT HOW GOOD OR HOW MUCH BETTER RUN YOUR COMPANY IS THAN YOUR COMPETITOR'S.*

If your customers start telling you about what a fine business operation you have, you're leaving something on the table. The only time your customer will tell you what a fine job you're doing and what a great company you have is when they're trying to encourage you to keep on doing what you've been doing -- *underpricing.*

Have you ever bragged to anybody about what a great job they were doing -- *to their face?* The only reason you ever brag on anybody *to their face* is that you're trying to pull off *positive reinforcement* (that's what they call it in the psychological literature). Let them know how wonderful you think they are doing and they will keep on doing it.

Just as an example, have you ever taken your kids out to a nice restaurant for lunch or dinner? Fancy place, you know, waiters in black suits, the whole ball of wax. Your daughter's 8, your son's 6. Nobody cries, nobody spills any milk, nobody kicks anybody, nobody fights. (This is a fairy tale.) And at the end of the meal when you are driving home, you say, "Hey kids, I was really proud of you." Now why are you bragging on them to them? *Because you want them to keep on doing it!* Now, next week, same kids, same restaurant. While they only spill one glass of milk, you are most upset because your son punched your daughter resulting in a loud, ear-splitting response. Later in the meal, your daughter, determined to get even, throws a spoonful of mashed potatoes at her brother and hits the lady at the next table. You still bragging about your kids on the way home?

The only reason your customers are going to tell you about what a "fine business" you've got is if they're trying to keep you doing what you've been doing. Now, to be sure, once in a while somebody might say, "Thanks, I appreciate what you did." and not be trying to con you. That's reasonable. But if you ever have lots of your customers telling you what a fine operation you've got, your prices are probably a little too low. Truth is, you really don't need to put up with that kind of talk. Raise your price and see how fast it stops.

• *GENERAL ABSENCE OF ANY COMPLAINTS ABOUT PRICE.*

If nobody's complaining about price, your prices are too low. You're leaving something on the table. There ought to be somebody gasping and choking at your price. People who teach purchasing agents how to buy teach them to flinch. Some will flinch no matter what. If *nobody's* flinching, your prices are too low.

- *PRICE HAS NOT BEEN CHANGED OVER A LONG PERIOD OF TIME, PARTICULARLY DURING KNOWN INFLATIONARY PERIODS.*

If you cut your price X% (say 2%), you have to do Y% more volume just to make up for the 2% price-cut. If you don't raise your prices for a year and inflation is 2%, what have you done? You've taken a *de facto* 2% price-cut. We have not had a period without inflation in the United States since the late 1920's. We've always had inflation in most working peoples' lifetimes. This means that we must raise prices regularly.

If you are too lily-livered to raise your price during inflationary times, you are, in essence, taking a price-cut. Very few people who will be reading these words were even alive during the last known period of deflation in the United States. Just remember, if you want to stay on the boards and make some money, you better be prepared to be a little bit aggressive on price. This means you have to raise it on a regular basis.

- *CUSTOMERS BUY WITHOUT HAGGLING PRICE, OR EVEN ASKING ABOUT WHAT IS OR IS NOT INCLUDED IN THE PRICE, OR DON'T EVEN ASK THE PRICE.*

If your customers call you up and just say, "Ship me a couple of these." or "Why don't you send over 4 dozen of those." or "I want to order this." your prices are too low. If everybody trusts you to charge a "fair" price, your prices are too low. What is a "fair" price? For most people, a "fair" price is the price they paid when they felt they got one hell-of-a-deal. If your customers *know* you charge a "fair" price, your prices are too low.

If you really want to know what a "fair" price is, I'll tell you. It's the price that is charged when *both* people feel they got taken. If there is ever a "fair" price, both sides will figure they "got took". If your customer knows you're going to be fair with them, that surely means they feel you are leaving a lot on the table. When a customer says, "Oh, I know you'll be fair." it should be taken as an insult. If your customer feels they don't have to ask the price, they can trust you to be fair, you are known as a low price vendor. They should at least be concerned enough about your price to inquire about it -- perhaps not paranoid, but at least reasonably alert to what your prices are; just enough to "keep you honest" as they say, just distrusting enough to ask, "Now what is that going to cost me?"

- *YOU'RE GETTING MANY NEW CUSTOMERS FOR NO APPARENT REASON OR EFFORT ON YOUR PART.*

If you suddenly start getting lots of new customers, and you haven't been out there beating the bushes, advertising and promoting -- they're just kind of swarming in through the door -- *your prices are too low.* That's the "thundering herd beating a path to your door" syndrome again. That's the better mousetrap at work.

The world is not going to beat a path to your door because you have a better product. The world is going to beat a path to your door *because the price on your product is too low.* Did People Express have a better product (service)? Or did they just have too low a price? Did Laker Airlines have a better product (service), or too low a price? When the "thundering herd is beating a path to your door", try raising your prices. They'll go away and leave you alone when you get your prices too high.

- *YOU HAVE A SUDDEN UPSURGE IN BUSINESS VOLUME, PARTICULARLY FROM NEW CUSTOMERS.*

If you suddenly start getting new customers and/or if old customers suddenly start buying more from you, that tells you that the word is out that they can get a good deal from you -- probably too good a deal. Think! The only reason you are going to get many new customers for no apparent reason -- or that several customers who have been buying from you for a long time (but who use more than one source) would start buying *more* from you -- is that they're probably buying less from your competition because your prices are too low.

- *YOUR CUSTOMERS INSIST THAT IF THERE IS FAULTY OR DEFECTIVE PRODUCT, YOU HAVE TO MAKE THE PRODUCT WORK OR REPLACE IT, RATHER THAN REFUND THEIR MONEY.*

One of the things that almost assuredly indicates that your prices are too low can be discerned from the way your customers behave whenever there's a problem of defective product. There is a basic principle that is virtually never

109

violated by customers. If someone buys a product, and *feels they received a really good deal*, but they find something wrong with it, they will want you to repair, replace or exchange the product. After all, "A deal is a deal, and you have to make it right." But if they buy something, and then find that maybe *they paid too much*, they usually will want their money back. "No, it's not any good, and another one probably isn't any good either. Just give me my money back."

Do you want to develop a substantive record to show you when your prices are too high or too low? Try this: Whenever there is a customer complaint about your product or service, write down the name of the customer, the product and what the customer *demanded* that you do about it. Here's why: Price-buyers tend to do the most complaining. You can identify products and/or services on which your prices are too low just by keeping such a log and periodically evaluating the frequency that certain items appear on it. Also, by keeping track of the customers who complain, you can start paying attention to what they buy. This is particularly valuable for wholesalers, distributors and retailers who sell a large variety of products. You'll find that the customers who begin to assemble in the "complainers group" will tend to buy only some specific items, but never buy other items. What does that tell you? The products they are buying are probably priced a little low.

You also want to keep a record of what your customers demanded that you do about their complaint. Their demands can be classified in one of two varieties: (1) money back (discount, refund, credit memos, etc.) or (2) replacement (repair, exchange, etc.). When a customer wants money back, virtually always it's because they feel they've paid too much. Your prices may be too high on those items. But when they want you to repair, replace or exchange it, your prices could be too low.

If you log customer complaints, you will notice that a pattern inevitably will begin to emerge. If you will keep such an on-going record and analyze it, you will find that your customer's behavior will tell you when your prices are too high or too low on various products and services.

• *LABOR AND MATERIALS COSTS HAVE INCREASED WITHOUT INCREASES IN YOUR PRICES.*

If your labor or materials costs begin to increase, especially if you're a manufacturer (but even if you're a retailer, wholesaler, distributor, contractor or whatever) and your prices don't go up, obviously your margins will begin shrinking. That means you are going to have to raise prices or your company will probably begin to have trouble meeting payroll and other expenses. Remember, maintaining your gross margin is an absolute necessity if you and/or your company are to remain in business.

• *A KNOWN PRICE-BUYER STARTS BUYING FROM YOU.*

You should always try to identify a few known price-buyers. The good news is they are almost always easily identified. They are the ones that really hammer you on price. If a known price-buyer places an order with you, your prices are probably too low on those items or services. So you occassionally want to really *try* to sell to a price-buyer -- not because you really expect to get an order, but to make a PRICE CHECK. Understand this: If you get an order from a known price-buyer, you have found out that your prices are too low!

As stated in Chapter 5, price-buyers take all your sales time. And I advise any sales rep who's trying to earn a good living not to spend much time making calls on price-buyers. Just head on down the road when you've got a real price-buyer who is just wasting your time. But remember this, *once in a while*, you really need to try to sell a price-buyer just to make a price check.

Here's the way to do it. Don't call on known price-buyers very often. And when you do call on them, don't ever give them a better price; just give them your *real* price -- the same deal that you're giving anybody and everybody else. Do this just to see if they'll buy at those prices because, if *they* buy, that tells you that your prices are too low on what they buy.

This effort at checking the correctness of your price should not be considered unethical, and the sales rep shouldn't feel that he/she is using someone or taking advantage of someone's time. After all, most price-buying customers will willingly waste *your* time and effort. They will ask you for a quote or a bid just to make their own price check -- perhaps just to keep the guy they're intending to buy from "honest". They don't feel that there is anything wrong with that -- even when it costs *you* perhaps thousands of dollars in time and effort to work up your bid or quote. They feel that's just part of your "cost of doing business". Thus, you ought to be able to make a price check just as well as your customer.

A buddy of mine in Phoenix refers to price-buyers as bird-dogs. He operates a ladies clothing store and we were in his store one day looking at some displays he was having installed and a woman comes in his store. When he saw her he said to me, "See that lady over there? She's one of our bird-dogs."

Well, I thought he was going to tell a joke, so I said, "Oh, yeah, how's that?"

He said, "Yeah, she's one of our pointers."

I'm not catching on and say, "What are you talking about?"

He said, "I'm sorry, Larry, that's just what I call some of our shoppers. She comes in here all the time. Never buys anything. I'm so pleased."

I said, "Why would that please you if she doesn't buy anything?"

He said, "Larry, if she ever came in here and pulled anything off the rack and carried it over to the cashier to pay for it, we would have incontrovertible evidence that our price on that item is the lowest price to be had anywhere in the world. And you know what, we don't even have to pay her to do that research; she works at it full time and has never made a mistake."

- *YOU HAVE A BIG BACKLOG OF DEMAND, PARTICULARLY IF YOUR BACKLOG OF DEMAND EXCEEDS THE AVERAGE FOR THOSE IN YOUR INDUSTRY OR WITH WHOM YOU COMPETE.*

If your customers have to wait longer to receive products from you, than to receive product from your competition, your prices are probably too low. Look at it like this. If your customers are willing to wait three or four weeks to get something from you, and are willing to do so when they could get it from your competitors in a week and a half, what's that tell you? *Everybody* wants it yesterday. If your customer is willing to wait longer to get something from you when they can get it quicker from your competitor, it is because your deal is sweeter. Your prices are too low.

**Reprinted with special permission
of King Features Syndicate, Inc.**

Some readers will say: "No, it is because our quality is so much better." Well, if your quality is so much better, why don't you charge more? To be sure, you don't want to drive off all your business, but willingness to wait for late delivery of "better quality" may very well dissipate when the price of that "better quality" goes up a little bit more. You see, if your customer prefers to wait longer for you to deliver, that waiting time is already a premium that they're willing to pay because you're so much better (cheaper). I'll bet if you raised the price just a little more some of that willingness to wait just might go away. Again, this is a way to test your price. Just check your backlog of orders compared to your competitor's backlog of orders, time-wise, and it will tell you if you are too low.   Your order backlog, time-wise, should never exceed your competitor's order backlog.

How can you find out about your competitor's backlog? Easy, just call them and say, "Hey, how long does one have to wait to get a shipment of whatever?" You'll find that most will be happy to give you the information. For those of you who sell for manufacturers, getting such information is particularly critical, but it is also important for those who rep for wholesalers, distributors and even retailers, depending upon what you're selling.

• *CUSTOMERS BUY MORE THAN THEY NEED AND YOU KNOW IT.*

What does it mean if your customers buy more than they need? There are only a few reasons your customer will buy more than they need: (1) They can't pay for it and want to load up before you find that out. (2) They are afraid they won't be able to get it in the future. (3) They are afraid prices will rise, and they want to get it on hand before they do.

The way to handle all three of these reasons is to raise your prices! Look at it this way: (1) If you are not going to get paid for it, you may as well charge more. (2) If customers are afraid they are not going to get it and start hoarding, you can stop their hoarding by raising prices. (3) If they are buying more than they need in anticipation of raising prices, they have just told you they think your prices already should be higher.

• *YOUR COMPANY'S BAD DEBT COLLECTION PROCEDURES ARE INCREASING IN ACTIVITY.*

If you suddenly start spending more time collecting money that is owed to you, it could be that your prices are too low. Here's why: if your average day's receivables (collection period) begin to increase, it may be because you have become attractive to price-buyers. There's only three reasons why your average day's receivables will increase. One reason is the economy's turning sour and nobody's paying their bills as fast. If that's the cause, you'll read about it in the newspaper. The second reason is because whoever does your credits and collections has gotten lazy. I must assume that you don't tolerate that in your business. That leaves us with the third reason: You've gotten attractive to people who are slower payers -- i.e., to price-buyers.

If the economy hasn't gotten sour, and if you are just as aggressive on collecting your receivables, then if your day's receivables begin to increase, timewise, you've probably gotten attractive to price-buyers. If that's the case, what do you want to do? Well, first, you want to take a look at your *new* customers. Because your new customers, in all likelihood, are the price-buyers that are running up your average collection time. Once you've identified these price- buyers, look at what they buy. In that way, your price-buyers will point to those items on which your prices are too low.

Now, you might say, "My job's selling; my job's not monitoring receivables." I understand that and that's why it's necessary to learn how to delegate. The job of the sales rep isn't to operate as an island or in a vacuum. You have to operate as an integrated whole with the rest of your business. Many sales reps think, "My job is to go out there and get orders. I'm not concerned about receivables unless it's on sales I made (and then I'm only concerned if I'm not going to get a commission until they pay)." Astute sales reps aren't so short-sighted. As a sales rep, you need to learn to be concerned about receivables because they can certainly identify areas where your prices are too low.

• *YOU'RE GETTING YOUR COMPETITOR'S CREDIT CUT-OFF BUSINESS.*

If you are getting your competitor's credit cut-off business, your prices are probably too low. Price-buyers are not only slower payers, they often become *no* payers after a while. If your competitors have refused credit to a customer and they come to you, you need to raise your price. If a price-buyer comes to you after he/she has been cut off from credit elsewhere, you may not have the lowest price in town, but you're probably next in line. There's no point in getting an order from somebody who isn't going to pay their bill. If you are getting your sales volume increases from customers who are struggling to stay in business, you aren't going to be gaining any profitable sales.

• *YOU KNOW YOUR CUSTOMER'S GROSS MARGIN, IT IS GETTING BIGGER, AND YOUR PRODUCT REPRESENTS A SIGNIFICANT PORTION OF YOUR CUSTOMER'S COST-OF-GOODS-SOLD.*

I keep emphasizing gross margin in this book. The reason is because gross margin is the basic signal of the life-blood of a company, just like your pulse indicates some basics about your body. No pulse, no life. No gross margin, no wages, salaries, commissions, or profits.

If you sell to other businesses, you should learn to monitor their gross margin because that will tell you when to tactically and strategically raise your prices. Few sales reps ever think in terms of strategy and tactics when it comes to pricing, especially when it comes to raising (or lowering) prices. There is a propituous time to raise prices, and that is not necessarily (or even usually) annually, or every spring or "whenever our costs go up". It is a function of doing it at the right time. And that right time is *always* when your customer's gross margin and sales volume is increasing -- when he's getting fat, when he's making money. What is the sure-fire indicator that he's making money? His gross-margin is increasing, particularly if his sales volume is increasing.

We saw this phenomenon several years ago in the auto industry. Remember when they were making those embarrassingly high profits; when all the big auto companies were giving those million dollar bonuses to their executives? The auto companies knew they were prime targets for price increases, so they said, "Absolutely no price increases." They stiff-armed their vendors, many of whom said, "Oh, okay. You will tell us when we can raise prices, won't you?" And the companies answered, "You bet, but not now, not now."

But the people who knew what they were doing simply passed along a price increase anyway. They knew that the auto companies would never tell them, "Okay, now is the time to raise price -- stick it to us." There is never a right time for you to raise prices in the eyes of your customer. Thus, those who made money looked at the auto companies' gross margins and knew they could get away with it. Automobile sales volume was increasing and the auto companies' gross margins were going up. This was the time to hit them for a price increase.

Like Yogi said, much can be observed by just watching. Pay attention. There is a time to raise prices, and your customer will tell you when that time arrives if you'll watch his gross margin and sales volume. The difference between a pro and an amateur in anything -- sports, selling, or whatever -- is that pros really study what they're doing. I don't care if it's their golf swing or their baseball swing, their backhand, their downhill skiing or the prices they are charging. If you're really a pro, you *know* when you can go after the price increase.

- *GUT FEELING, YOU JUST PLAIN DON'T FEEL YOUR PRICES ARE TOO HIGH.*

If your gut feeling just tells you "maybe we can do better", I'd recommend that you raise prices. Intuition does play a role in pricing. Some people seemingly just have a feel for knowing when they can get away with a higher price. But a lot of sales people *don't* because it has never even occurred to some that their prices may be too low, being (dis)content in the knowledge that their prices are *always* too high.

- *YOUR REQUEST FOR QUOTATIONS ACTIVITY INCREASES DRAMATICALLY.*

This point is particularly important for anyone who works in a bid situation because if you want to sell (through bidding) at top dollar -- you will need to keep a perennial record of your "RFQs" (Requests for Quotations). If, in a normal week, you are asked to bid six times, and then you suddenly find that you're asked to make eight quotes per week, one of two things are happening: (1) either the economy's picking up (which, again, you'll read about in the newspaper) or (2) your prices are too low and the word's out on the street. If your RFQ activity is increasing, and everybody else's is too, your prices aren't necessarily too low. But don't forget that when business is booming, demand (necessarily) is high and climbing, and you should be aggressively raising prices anyway -- i.e., the time is right. If your RFQ activity is increasing, but nobody else's is, then there seems to be a genuine preference of those customers to buy from you rather than someone else -- and there's a good chance that it's because your price is too low.

- *YOUR SUCCESS RATE ON WINNING JOBS YOU BID ON SIGNIFICANTLY INCREASES.*

Another indicator that your prices are too low in bid situations occurs when your success rate on winning jobs that you bid on begins increasing dramatically. If you normally get 1 out of 4 jobs that you bid on and, all of a sudden, you find that you're getting 1 out of 3, again you can suspect that your prices are too low.

A good example of this can be seen by studying contractors who have survived in the construction business. Those that I know who have continuously made money invariably look at the win/lose percentage of the contracts that they bid on. And when their success ratio begins to increase, the first thing they check on is whether they are making mistakes in estimating. Did we forget the other half of the roof, or something like that? Then they'll check out the take-offs, the estimates and so forth. And if they don't find mistakes, then they figure, "Our prices are too low. We are winning more than our *fair share*. Maybe we have been sharpening our pencils a little too much."

Incidentally, a parallel can be seen here for people who don't sell in bid situations. A lot of sales people are terrified of losing a sale -- *any* sale. If you want to sell at a high price, you'll have to learn that you must lose some sales, for you will never know your prices are high enough until you lose some sales. And the only way to do that is to *test* your prices. The nice thing about bidding is you can test your price *every* time you submit a quote. When one sells off a price-list, it can get a bit expensive testing prices -- printing new price-lists every day can cost big dollars.

Incidentally, while we are talking about losing some sales, a word to the wise about market share. If you have a 25% market share, that means you *better* lose, on the average, 3 out of 4 jobs that you bid (assuming that all four jobs were the same size). When you strive to increase market share, there is a chance that your company will do that by "buying" the business. This is not always a smart thing to do. Improving market share through sale of the right quality stuff, delivered on time, and backed up with good service will be profitable. But increasing market share at the expense of declining gross margin might put you on the track of becoming the biggest company in your business to file for bankruptcy. (See Chapter 1 for names of several of the world's largest companies that have accomplished that feat.)

• *YOU'RE TEMPTED TO SELL AT A HIGHER PRICE THAN YOU'RE ASKING OR QUOTING.*

Temptation is an interesting thing. A lot of people fight it. But one temptation that you ought to succumb to is the temptation to raise prices. If you are tempted to, give it a try-out. The worst you can do is lose a sale. *You'll never know if your price is high enough until you test it.*

Personally, I would far rather sell in a bid situation than off a price-list because you can test your price with every job you quote, every day, and judge what percentage you win. That information tells you something, and puts you in an environment where you can test your price every day and know what you're doing, rather than have to live with a published price-list or catalogue for six months to a year or more. If you do your homework in a bid situation, you're going to know how you're doing all the time.

Remember, as we said at the outset of this book - *YOU* cut your price, *YOU* write those numbers down, *YOU* slit your throat. Your competition isn't the one that quotes your price, YOU DO. If you are too low, too often, only one result -- sooner or later -- is going to happen. That is why you must *test* your price.

• *YOUR CUSTOMER WOULD LIKE TO WORK FOR YOU AS A SALES REP.*

I throw this one in just for fun. But there is some truth to it that merits consideration for I know of some situations where buyers have asked sales reps if the sales rep's company, "needs any help selling?" Translation: "Anybody being paid commission can earn a great living (for a while) at the prices you guys charge. It may not last forever because the company will probably go broke pretty quick, but in the near term you must be picking up some pretty easy commissions." Again, your customer will alert you to the fact that your prices are too low.

• *YOUR COMPETITOR'S REPS START COMPLAINING TO YOUR CUSTOMERS ABOUT YOU AND HOW YOU DO BUSINESS.*

If your competition starts complaining about you and the way you do business, your prices are probably too low. Why? Well, look at it like this. Have you ever complained about a competitor who charges higher prices than you do? If your competition starts complaining about the way you do business, you're hurting them. But you are also hurting yourself; you're leaving a lot on the table. I'm not sure I'd take any satisfaction from that.

- *A POTENTIAL DISTRIBUTOR FOR YOUR PRODUCTS IS ALREADY BOOTLEGGING YOUR PRODUCTS (OR, WORSE YET, RESELLING YOUR PRODUCT AT A HIGHER PRICE THAN YOUR REGULAR DISTRIBUTORS) AND/OR YOUR REGULAR DISTRIBUTORS ARE CHARGING FAR HIGHER PRICES THAN THEY WERE SUPPOSED TO.*

If you've got a product that you sell to someone who, in turn, resells the product to the end user, and you find out that someone who is *not* an authorized distributor is selling your product, guess what? Your prices are way too low. The only way this can occur is that this unauthorized distributor is able to obtain your product, pay the bootlegger (who is probably your customer unless your employees are stealing it from you), and still sell at a competitive price to your regular dealers and distributors -- and presumably make some money at it.

I know of a couple of incidents where this has happened, but I think the most telling example of how a manufacturer found out his price was too low occurred when this manufacturer was selling a product that had to be used in pairs. He sold it strapped together in pairs to his distributors with a suggested resale price of $150 for the pair. He discovered after a while that his very best distributor was only hitting about 70% of quota, while most were hitting quota, or even a little better. Even those with a poor track record were hitting quota. So he goes out and talks to this distributor, and he discovers that this distributor thought that the price of the product was $150 each and they simply came strapped together in pairs because the user had to use them in pairs. He was selling them for $300 for the pair -- and he was hitting 70% of quota. Guess what the manufacturer did? He raised the price.

A lot of funny things can happen in the distribution channel. And if you sell to wholesalers and distributors, and/or you are a wholesaler or distributor, you're in that channel. Study the other distributors and wholesalers. What do they sell; where do they get it? Look around. If an unauthorized distributor is bootlegging a product and competing with you, how can they do that financially? Consider what you can learn from the implications of what they are doing -- as well as thinking in terms of taking legal action against them.

120

- *COMPETITION BOWS OUT AND CAN'T COMPETE WITH YOU ANYMORE BECAUSE THEY WENT BROKE.*

"Hot dog! Ran them suckers right out-of-business." Don't ever come bragging to me about how you ran a competitor out-of-business. If you ever take any satisfaction from running your competition out-of-business, you probably made two major mistakes: (1) If you ran a competitor out-of-business, you're likely leaving a lot on the table. That's bad enough, but the other mistake is worse. (2) If you ran your competitor out-of-business, you probably have financially set up a *new* competitor to come into *your* business who can compete with you on a lower price basis.

This is especially true if you must use dedicated machinery and equipment in your business. Because when that competitor went broke, his assets were probably sold off in liquidation. That means somebody bought that dedicated machinery and equipment at liquidation value, and now you've just set up a new competitor to come in with far lower costs (and prices) with their newly purchased machinery and equipment.

For example, an airplane is a dedicated machine. Once you build an airplane, you may as well use it for an airplane. Who's flying People Express airplanes today? Who's flying Frontier Airline airplanes today? Or any of the airplanes of the 200+ airlines that have gone broke since airline deregulation? Or did they just throw all those airplanes out in the ocean when those companies went bankrupt? I'll tell you who is flying them. Some of the old, existing carriers who snapped them up cheap, and some of the (as of the date of this writing) 215 newly started airlines which started up subsequent to airline deregulation in 1978.

If you run a competitor out-of-business, you probably left some on the table in the process; but worse yet, you have probably caused them to sell off any dedicated machinery and equipment which they had. This machinery and equipment will almost assuredly be put back into competition against you, which means that you're even going to have more price competition. Don't ever price to try to run competition out-of-business. The only time that strategy works is if you are certain that you can buy that machinery and equipment from

121

him -- and if you ran him out-of-business, it may be a cold day in hell before he lets *you* get your hands on it.

- *YOUR CUSTOMERS QUIT BUYING FROM YOU AND THEN THEY COME BACK.*

This is the most difficult concept for sales people to grasp, and it is essential to understand it if you are ever going to sell at a high price, especially if you are ever going to slam dunk a sale. Again, the principle is: *if you ever lose a customer, and then they come back to you, your prices are too low.* This is particularly true if there was a bitter scene: if they said unkind things about your mother's nocturnal habits, referred to you as the south end of a northbound horse, and said they would *never* buy from you again.

If you ever lose a customer, and then they come back to you, you must question *why* they came back? The answer usually is because they went out and they checked everybody in town, every vendor they could find, and they found out that you have the best deal. Your prices are lower than anybody else's (compared to the quality, service and delivery you give). This tells you it's time to raise those prices.

- *THE PRINCIPLE OF SHANE.*

Some 40 or so years ago there was a movie titled <u>Shane</u>. This is a classic western in which Alan Ladd plays the title role. The most famous scene is the last scene where Shane is riding off into the sunset and the little kid is chasing after him yelling "Shane, come back Shane!"

What's that got to do with selling? Plenty. Don't *ever* chase a customer. If you ever have a customer "walk" on you -- "I can get it down the street, cheaper." -- *let him go!!* Chasing him, yelling, "Shane, come back Shane," is a stupid waste of time. *Let him go!!* If he is a price-buyer (like he says he is), and he buys strictly on price (like he says he does), the only way you will stop him from going out the door is if you give him a price so low that he feels there is no point in shopping other sources -- i.e., a price so low that he knows he can't possibly do any better -- the *lowest* price in town.

Let him go. Because when he goes, he will be doing research for you. Absolutely thorough, methodical and accurate research concerning the value of what you have to offer *vis a vis* the value of every competitor of yours that he can find.

The principle of Shane is this: If Shane ever comes back, *your last quote was too low*. For if Shane comes back, by evidence of his return, he is saying (no matter what he actually says), "Sir, Shane reporting in. I just went out and checked every deal I could find from your competitors and it looks like yours is the best deal. Is that last quote still good?" The answer to that is, "NO! Since we last talked that price has gone up (10%, $200, whatever)."

- *YOU -- THE SALES REP -- (A) GRAB THE LUNCH CHECK, (B) PAY CASH, (C) DO NOT NEED ANY RECEIPTS, AND (D) DON'T WANT ANY MORE COMMISSION CHECKS THIS TAX YEAR.*

This one is a bit facitious and you may not see the humor but the point is: if sales reps are getting real fat and making tons of money, but the company's not making any money, prices are too low. Now I know the people reading this are mostly sales reps, and you'd like to get real fat and, confidentially, you don't care if the company makes any money. You may feel that way *until* the company files for bankruptcy.

Then, not only do you have to look for another job, but you probably won't get any commissions that are still due you. Commissions aren't wages. When you have a bankruptcy, commissions usually don't get paid. That's when you might learn the difference between 1099 income and W-2 wages. Of course, maybe you will make a lot between now and the time the company goes belly-up. But you can be assured that if you're getting fat at the expense of the company's operating profits, the slack will come out of the chain. They will either wise-up and cut your commissions, or file for bankruptcy.

- *A COMPETITOR OF YOURS WANTS TO BUY FROM YOU AND (A) SAYS HE CAN'T MAKE A SHIPPING SCHEDULE AND (B) WANTS YOU TO PRIVATE LABEL, ESPECIALLY IF PRODUCING THE PRODUCT REQUIRES TOOLING ON YOUR PART.*

Can you afford to sell to a competitor? If you have a competitor who can afford to buy from you (at your prices) and resell to someone else, you have a sales and marketing problem and/or your prices are too low. I run across businesses who sell to their competition, but in most cases, I can't figure out why. It's understandable if you're selling to a competitor who can sell in a market that

123

you're precluded from (because of the law or something). But I can't understand how a company can possibly sell to a competitor who's selling to a customer that is fair game in the marketplace. If you're prohibited from selling in Noplaceland, and you have a competitor who's authorized to sell in Noplaceland, you might sell to them. That makes sense. But if you sell to a competitor who sells to customers you can and should be selling to, your prices are too low or you have a sales/marketing problem. Why can't you reach that customer? And/or how can the competitor who buys from you and can afford to pay your price still (presumably) profit by selling to a (should be) customer of yours?

- *THE CUSTOMER COMES TO YOUR OFFICE WITH A .357 MAGNUM, POINTS IT SQUARELY BETWEEN YOUR EYES, AND SAYS, "YOU HAVE TO QUOTE THIS JOB BECAUSE I WANT YOU TO HAVE IT."*

If your customer makes it really easy for you to sell to him, your prices are too low. If a customer comes to your office and insists on you making a bid or a quote, your prices are too low. There may be even other, more sinister reasons that they want a quote so badly from you, but if they're waiting on the curb for you to come to work in the morning, or if they're climbing in over the transom when you're closing up at night saying, "Hey, you know, we didn't get a bid from you yet, and we need one so you can get the work," it's because they know your bid will be lower than anyone else's.

- *THE CUSTOMER ASKS, "IS THIS PRICE LIST STILL IN EFFECT?" OR, "IS THIS QUOTE STILL GOOD?"*

The answer is "no". That's right, "NO".

Whenever a customer asks, "Is this price list still in effect? Is this quote still good? Is this bid still good?" the answer is no. The only reason anyone would ask you if this quote is still good is because they *cannot believe* that this quote is still good. But they will ask on the off-chance you're dumb enough to say, "Yes". They may as well take a shot at it. Putting it that way is far better than saying, "I'm sure this price isn't in effect anymore, is it?" and thereby alerting you to the fact that they think your prices are too low.

CHAPTER 12

INDICATORS OF
OVERPRICING

*"What are you going to say when
they ask about your price?"
Answer: "Look hurt."
Sporting goods salesman in Texas*

It is possible to overprice a product, to be sure. But overpricing is a far less common practice than is underpricing. As mentioned above, most people are so terrified that their prices are too high, they never even come close to pushing their prices as high as they ought to be. They certainly never test their price in any meaningful sense. Virtually always, they're so *certain* that they'll lose *all* their sales that they won't even sample the waters and try raising their price.

Yet many people have discovered, albeit inadvertently, that by raising prices their sales volume actually increases as a consequence, rather than declines. To be sure, when someone raises their price, they usually lose some sales. But, as pointed out in Chapter 9, you can afford to lose some sales and still make more money by raising prices. The question is not so much one of will you probably lose some sales; the question is will you lose so many sales that you'll lose profitability to the firm and income for the people that work there.

We certainly know that printing errors occur in magazines, newspapers and, to be sure, in advertisements, catalogues and published price-lists. What happens when someone makes a mistake and publishes a *too high* price in a direct mail catalogue? There is no real opportunity to correct that price, short of publishing an errata sheet. And if the erroneous price is not caught before the catalogue is distributed, there is no meaningful way to correct the price at all. One just has to live with it. Yet, people in the catalogue and direct mail business can give numerous examples of where the wrong price was printed; the price was entirely too high compared to what the price was supposed to be; and yet sales volume, in many cases, increased over what was projected. In even more cases, even though there was not a gain in sales, the normal sales volume was maintained.

Another point should be recognized when it comes to worrying about whether your prices are too high. Many business people feel they have competitors down the street who are always 2% below their price. And they've noticed that when they lower their price 5% or 10% or whatever percent, their competition lowers their price the same amount and still manages to be 2% lower than they are. Yet these same people don't seem to realize that if they would raise their price, that competitor who is 2% lower than they are, almost always raises their price by the same amount and *still* are only 2% lower. The only sure-fire solution to obtaining a reasonably high, profitable price for selling your products and services is to be willing to test your price and see what happens when efforts are made to sell at a higher price. The ability to sell at a higher price, of course, is a function of your selling skill because there is no *right* or *correct* price.

BUT I REALLY THINK MY PRICES ARE TOO HIGH

The foregoing notwithstanding, there certainly is a possibility that your prices are too high. And just as there are indicators that your prices are too low, there are indicators that your prices may be too high on your products or services. Perhaps a brief look at some of the major indicators of overpricing is warranted for purposes of completeness in this book.

• *YOUR COMPETITORS' PRICES ARE LOWER THAN YOURS.*
If your competitors' prices are lower than yours, it is possible that your prices are too high. Of course, the basic thesis of this book is that you fully expect your

competitors' prices to be lower than yours. Just because your competitors' prices are lower than yours does not mean your prices are too high. And even if everybody's prices are lower than yours, it is still not an indicator that your prices are too high. Certainly, however, if you have other competitors whose prices are as high or higher than yours, it is doubtful that your prices are too high. But if all your competitors' prices are lower than yours, perhaps your prices are too high.

•   *YOUR GROSS PROFIT PERCENTAGE IS GROWING -- BUT YOUR SALES ARE NOT.*

A second indicator that your prices may be too high (or perhaps have gotten too high with your last price increase) can occur when your gross margin or gross profit percentage starts growing but your sales volume begins to decline. As pointed out before, your gross margin or gross profit is that percentage of the sales dollar that is left after you have paid for what you sold. The only way gross profit can decline is because your sales price is too low relative to your costs. Likewise, the only way your gross profit can increase is because your costs are too low relative to your prices. Therefore, increasing gross profit or gross margin percentages can be an indicator that your prices are too high. But this increase in your gross margin had better be the result of higher prices *coupled with a decline in your sales volume.* If you raise your price and you actually sell more, you'll not only be experiencing an increasing gross margin but increasing sales volume, and you'll have a whopping big increase in your operating profit and your ability to pay the people that work in the firm. This is not an unheard-of phenomenon, particularly when people have been charging too low a price to begin with. Therefore, if your gross profit percentage is growing and your sales are not declining and/or if your sales actually are increasing, this would definitely not be an indicator that your prices are too high. However, it is possible that your prices are too high if you experience an increasing gross profit margin with declining sales. Just be sure that the declining sales are more than offsetting the increase in gross profit dollars which could still cause the firm, and the people working there, to realize as much or more profitability on the declining sales.

- *YOU RECEIVE MANY CUSTOMER COMPLAINTS (OR INQUIRIES) ABOUT WHAT IS OR IS NOT INCLUDED IN YOUR PRICE.*

Naturally, your customers will tell you that your prices are too high. Sales people will also complain that the company's prices are too high, but this is not a valid test of overpricing. In fact, many experienced sales managers will argue that the sure-fire indicator that a businesses' prices are too low is when the sales people quit complaining that their prices are too high.

You should take it as a given that your customers and sales reps will complain that your prices are too high. But an indicator that your prices (perhaps) really are too high is when those making inquiries about your price directly ask about what is or what is not included in your price. For example, if your customer thinks your prices are too high, they will often ask, "What does that include?" Many times people will hear a price that they think is extremely high, but will almost always assume that the price is reasonable and, therefore, try to justify it. What they are trying to do in their own mind is to validate the reasonableness of your *seemingly* too high price.

One must read such inquiries very carefully to adequately determine that the customer is, in fact, trying to validate the *correctness* of the price. For example, if a travel agent says that a trip to a vacation spot is $1000, the customer might ask, "Does that include lodging?" or, "Does that include airfare?" or even, "Does that include meals?". If someone is buying a coffee mug and the clerk says the price is $10, it would be doubtful that the customer would inquire, "Does that include delivery?" or "Does that include all taxes?", but they might ask, "Is it hand-painted?" or, "Is this made by a local artist?". The point is, when a price is perceived as being high, customers will try to verify the many dimensions of the price in trying to ascertain that it is somehow reasonable.

- *YOUR DOLLAR SALES VOLUME IS DECLINING.*

Another potential indicator that your prices are too high is you begin to experience a decline in sales volume. However, as we all know, sales volume can decline for a lot of reasons. One of those reasons is lack of sales effort. A second reason, of course, can be lack of promotional and advertising activity. Yet a third reason can be a consequence of the economy, and still further reasons can be a set of new competitors in the marketplace, etc., etc.

Just because your dollar sales volume begins to decline does not mean that your prices are too high. However, one should look at timing relative to this question. If you raise prices and your dollar sales volume begins to decline, it may indicate that your prices are too high. This is especially true if you are studying the other marketplace indicators which impinge upon the sales volume that you might be expected to do, and nothing has changed except your price.

HIGHER PRICES, HIGHER SALES[17]

Many CEO's are scared to death of pricing their products higher than those of their competitors---even if the competing products aren't of equivalent quality or usefulness. Walter Riley, who heads G.O.D. Inc., knows the feeling. But his own experience with pricing strategy, he says, has taught him that you shouldn't be afraid to charge more if you're confident you're offering more. At G.O.D., an overnight freight business, a price boost was the key ingredient in a mix that led to meteoric growth. From its founding in 1983 until three years later, Riley kept his prices competitive with other truckers. "We were toe to toe with them," he says, "and we still weren't getting any new business." In 1986 the company began pricing at a 5%-to-7% premium, and the price change, along with a small acquisition, in one year brought sales from $3.8 million to $12.7 million. Charging a premium price, Riley says, meant instant credibility. It also differentiated G.O.D. from its competitors. "Raising our prices startled purchasing agents into seeing that we weren't just like our competitors. And they were willing to pay extra for overnight delivery."

---

17 Inc., October 1988, p. 112.

In the absence of any other reasons for your sales volume to be declining, and given that you simply raised prices in the reasonably near past, there may be grounds to believe that your prices are too high.

- ### *YOUR COMPETITIONS' SHARE OF THE MARKET IS INCREASING.*

If your competitors' market share is increasing, it is possible that your prices are too high. Or it may be an indicator that he's trying to "buy in" to the market. Many people believe that market share insures success in the marketplace. However, history really shows no such correlations and is replete with examples of the largest single competitors in a marketplace filing for bankruptcy. For example, in the past few years: the world's *largest retailer* filed for bankruptcy; the *second largest convenience food chain* in the United States filed for bankruptcy; the *largest public transportation company* in the United States filed for bankruptcy; the *largest retail grocery chain* filed for bankruptcy; the *largest bus company* filed for bankruptcy; the *largest cement manufacturer* filed for bankruptcy, etc., etc. Unfortunately the pursuit of market share has been touted as a source of success in business in many of our nation's leading business schools and learned journals. Consequently, many people believe that market share, per se, is the secret to success in business and blindly pursue it, assuming that profitability will necessarily emerge.

Let's face facts -- if market share assured success, General Motors wouldn't have the problems they have today. Thirty years ago General Motors' main concern was that they had *too much* market share and the Justice Department would break the company up. Today they worry about bankruptcy. A lot of good "owning the market" did them. Don't be so concerned about losing market share to your competition, particularly if your competitor is an idiot and is blindly trying to increase the company's market share. Remember it is better to be profitable at whatever volume of business you're doing, than to go broke while being the biggest guy in the business. You're just a bigger bust if you're the biggest in the business when you do go bust.

From a strategic standpoint, you should also think in terms of your share of the market relative to business volume. Almost always when business is turning down in a recessional cycle, one should necessarily gain market share. Likewise, when business is improving, one almost always loses market share. The reason for this, of course, is that in a business downturn many companies go out-of-business, and consequently those who stay in business find an increasing share of the market. Conversely, when business is expanding, more businesses enter the marketplace, and most all competitors in the marketplace lose some percentage share of the market as a consequence.

• *YOU ARE RECEIVING MANY PRICE COMPLAINTS.*

If you are receiving many complaints about your price, it is possible that your prices are too high. However, once again, be very cautious about locking on the number of price complaints and interpreting that as an indicator that your prices are too high. Many business people, especially sales people, receive price complaints *because they invite and encourage price complaints.* As we pointed out in Chapter 2, many sales reps encourage and invite price complaints by the way they handle the very issue of price itself. Lines such as, "Isn't it a crime the price they charge for this stuff?" or, "Do you think eight bucks would be too much?", invite price complaints from customers. It may be that your prices are too high and, of course, if your prices really are too high you will probably get a lot of price complaints. But be sure you are not inviting or causing those price complaints to occur.

• *WHENEVER THERE IS A REQUEST FOR AN ADJUSTMENT BECAUSE OF A FAULTY OR DEFECTIVE PRODUCT OR SERVICE, THE COMPLAINT IS ACTUALLY A DISGUISED PRICE COMPLAINT, RATHER THAN A TRUE COMPLAINT ABOUT THE QUALITY OF THE PRODUCT.*

When a customer has bought something from you, and the customer is not satisfied with that product or service, they may very well register a complaint. By studying these complaints, you can determine if, in fact, you are receiving a truly faulty or defective product or service complaint, or a complaint about price. Such a determination is easily made. Almost always when people complain about something that they bought, and they feel that the price was fair to them (meaning reasonably low), they will simply want you to repair, replace, exchange or somehow make good the product or service which they bought. "A

131

deal's a deal." However, if someone buys something and then discovers that they could have bought it cheaper from someone else, they almost always tell you that they want some kind of credit memo or a refund.

If one is truly interested in determining whether or not they are charging an adequately high price, they should maintain a record of all complaints about allegedly faulty or defective product or service provided their customers. They should not only record what the product or service was, but also the *demand* made by the customer to make it right. Such demands can be categorized as either some form of, "I want my money back," or, "I want you to repair/replace/exchange the product (or service)." If most of the complaints you get are to the effect that they want their money back, your prices are probably too high. On the other hand, if most of the complaints you get are for repair/replace/exchange, your prices are defintely not too high and are probably too low.

• *YOUR WHOLESALER BUYER ASKS SERIOUSLY, "IS THAT THE RETAIL PRICE?"*

If you sell to someone who resells your product, those people may indicate that your prices are too high. The way they do that is by seriously asking if the price you're quoting is the retail (resale) price. Again, if a customer who is going to resell your product is absolutely dumbfounded at your prices, this may be an indicator that your prices are too high. However, again, a warning is necessary here. If the customer is going to resell your product, they will probably feel that the more they can beat on you in an effort to get a lower price, the more that will facilitate their ability to resell the product at a lower price. One must be very cautious about interpreting the honesty of such statements by customers who intend to resell your product.

• *YOUR SALES REPS ASK, "IF I TAKE LESS COMMISSION, CAN I SELL AT A LOWER PRICE?"*

Sometimes sales reps truly face the situation where their prices are too high. And it is not unknown for sales reps to offer to take lower commissions in an effort to get a sale because they simply know that they're not going to get the sale at the price that they are currently asking. This situation most commonly emerges in large volume sale. I remember consulting with a company that sold furniture to hotels and motels. The sales rep had a lead on a sale for 500 rooms of furniture to a new hotel. He decided that, at the prices they were currently asking, they would not get the order; but if the company "got competitive" they could get the order for the entire 500 rooms of hotel furniture. The sales rep approached the boss and suggested that he was so certain of this fact that he would be willing to give up half his commission in order to lower the price adequately to get the sale. This practice was successful and probably did accurately indicate that the company's initial price was too high. It is less likely, however, that such tactics would work in very small order situations.

- *CUSTOMERS ARE CALLING THE OFFICE AND INQUIRING ABOUT YOUR PRICES OR TO "DOUBLE CHECK" YOUR PRICES.*

Yet another indicator that perhaps your prices are too high is if you have customers, or prospective customers, calling your office to verify, or double check, price quotations. Many times when someone receives a price that they perceive as outrageously high, particularly in a written quotation format, they will check with the head office to be sure that the quotation was accurate. Again, when such inquiries occur, whoever fields that inquiry should be very careful about automatically assuming that this is an indicator that their prices are too high. However, it is a possibility.

- *YOU HAVE A TOUGH TIME EXPLAINING YOUR PRICES.*

If you are out there negotiating and you have a tough time justifying your prices *vis a vis* your competitors' prices, it is possible that your prices are too high. Again, however, it is possible for the sales rep to invite and encourage price complaints and/or to be so stupid, lazy, unthinking or naive that they cannot adequately explain why it is that their product or service warrants a higher price because of superior quality, service, delivery, spare parts, customer service, etc. Simply having to answer questions as to why your price is higher than your competitor's price is not an indicator that your prices are too high. In fact, good sales reps who sell at high prices view that as an opportunity to suggest to the customer the very reasons that their prices are higher, and why the customer should buy from them at that higher price. However, if you seem to be unable to explain why your prices are warranted when they are significantly higher than your competition, it is possible that your sales prices are too high.

133

In summary, it is possible to have your prices too high. The foregoing points might indicate that your prices are not only higher than your competitors' prices, but are too high. However, always keep in mind that it is very difficult to charge too high a price. Your price actually becomes too high when you don't think it is warranted, and/or you cannot justify the reasonableness of your higher price because of your superior quality, service or delivery. You should also keep in mind that if you are going to be a viable competitor in the marketplace, you probably must charge a higher price than your competitor. The reason is that ultimately most businesses that do go broke do so cutting prices, and there is a high degree of probability that if you are in a viable business that your prices must be higher than some of your competitors' prices. The businesses that fail are almost always those which charge lower prices -- not those that charge a higher price.

CHAPTER 13

PURCHASING AGENT TRICKS
TO GET YOU TO
CUT YOUR PRICE

*"How can you advertise your
product as being the finest quality
if you buy cheap stuff?"*
Supplier to automotive industry

Several years ago I was working down in Tampa with a group of purchasing
agents, and they got to talking about how to beat-up on sales reps. They were
trading secrets on "tricks" they used to get sales reps to cut their prices. My
reaction was one of resentment, inasmuch as I have always been sales oriented.
I kind of had the feeling they were talking about my family in front of me and
didn't know it was my family they were talking about -- and not saying nice
things. I became a little uncomfortable and was about ready to leave when I got
to thinking I could pull the old "fox in the henhouse" trick; that maybe I could
write some of this stuff down and use it to help some of my sales buddies. In fact,
that's when I got the idea to develop all the material I have acquired over the
years on the subject of pricing and profitability.

I certainly haven't recorded all the tricks that customers use to beat-up sales reps on prices, but probably any veteran sales rep has encountered most all of these tricks at one time or another. This section is not intended to be a divine revelation; instead its purpose is to shed some light on what the sales rep can do when some of these situations occur.

●   *THEY STIFF-ARM THE REP.*

They stiff-arm the sales person by simply saying, "I can't pay any more," or, "I can only pay X amount." This tactic is designed just to get the sales rep to knuckle under, as if God, personally, had so decreed that amount.

The way you foil this trick is to say, "Why not?" or, "How did you come up with that figure?" The reason you respond with that is because they're going to say, "Because (somebody) said so." -- my boss, Mr. Jones, my Mommy, or whoever. When they say, "Because so and so said so," they're *fingering* the person with whom you can most effectively do your selling.

Any successful sales rep will learn that you sell to *decision makers* and people who *influence* decision makers. Sometimes it is hard to find out who those people are. When your customer says, "Because (so and so) said so," they are telling you who the real decision maker is.

Your next trick, of course, is figuring out how to get to that decision maker because, until you do, you can't really sell your quality, service or whatever it is that you feel is your competitive edge. And remember, you need to know what your competitive edge is so that you can sell on that basis. A purchasing agent's (or buyer's) job is often just to beat you up on the price once they've made sure they will get the right stuff -- on time. If you can deliver the right stuff -- on time -- and especially if your competition can't, you have to get to the decision maker to explain this to them. That's all part of salesmanship and it's known as back-door selling. So don't just lay down and die when your customer says, "We can't pay any more." Ask, "Why not?" and find out who it is you need to sell to.

●   *THEY IMPLY (OR FLATLY STATE) THAT YOUR COMPETITOR'S QUALITY, SERVICE AND DELIVERY IS AS GOOD OR BETTER THAN YOURS.*

When your customer says, "I can get the same stuff down the street from your competitor, and cheaper," your secret reaction to that must always be, "Why are you talking to me?" You don't say that, but you *ask and answer* that question yourself. Think: Why does my prospect say to me, "I can get just as good a deal (or better) down the road," why not just do it? The answer is, of course, because they can't, don't want to or better not. If, in fact, they could get a better deal down the street, they wouldn't spend any time telling you about it! They would just run you off and place their order with your competition.

How do you handle this trick? Waste some of your customer's time (professionally, of course). Why waste some of his time? Look at it this way: Your customers' time is valuable to them. If they knew of a better deal, they'd just take it. By spending time telling you about a better deal, they are actually signalling you that they (1) really can't get a better deal -- they're lying about the price or the other vendor can't deliver on time or refuses to sell to them (perhaps because they haven't paid their last bill); (2) can get the deal, but really don't want to (which means they prefer to buy from you and the grounds for that preference, of course, warrants a higher price to you); or (3) can get the deal but *better not* because so-and-so said so.

Even when your customer is telling you the truth -- that he can get just as good quality, service and delivery down the street from your competitor *at a lower price* -- it doesn't mean he *will* buy from them. It just means he's trying to get you to cut your price. What he is really saying, even then, is, "I want you and everything about you. I just want your competitor's price."

Your reaction to that must always be, "If you want everything about me, you pay my price. If you want my competitor's price, then you get him and everything about him: his lack of inventory, investment, parts, experience, his inability to deliver, his lack of warranty or guarantee, etc." Remember what we said: Oftentimes purchasing agents will lie (or exaggerate just a little) about the other guy's deal. Furthermore they are often told *what* to buy and/or *from whom* to buy it. For a multiplicity of reasons -- and who knows what those reasons may be -- a purchasing agent may have to (or badly need to) buy from you. But they are still apt to say, "I can get it cheaper down the road," in the hopes that you will be obliging and cut your price.

137

Remember this subtle point, too: If your customers really spend a lot of time talking to you about the better deal they can get down the street, they not only may *want* to buy from you, they may *have* to buy from you. Why? Because your competitor *won't sell to him!* Maybe your customer hasn't paid his last bill, or he is just too hard to do business with, or he pays but it is just too much trouble to get him to pay or to comply with his silly rules or paperwork. (For example, one study showed that as many as 25% of the businesses in the United States will not sell to the U.S. Government just because of the problems in paperwork and trying to get paid.)

- *THEY SAY, "LET'S WRITE IT UP AT A LOWER PRICE THIS TIME. WE'LL SEE IF WE CAN'T PAY MORE LATER WHEN WE KNOW HOW WELL YOU CAN PERFORM."*

Let's analyze this one. This argument by your customer is, on one hand, a simple admission that they *do* pay more for good quality, service and delivery (why else do you have to be at a *lower* price than the vendor they are buying from *now* unless they are tacitly admitting that *proven* better performance is worth something more) and, on the other hand, a sucker ploy.

Look at it this way: If you can do it once (sell at a low price), you can do it again, and again, and again. Don't ever fall for this sucker line that, "You can get your foot in the door," or, "We can get things rolling." This whole sucker pitch preys upon notions that a lot of economists talk about called *marginal pricing* or *incremental pricing* or *going after the marginal customer.* Remember what we said before about why you don't mess with price-buyers. Reason #4 was, "They will tell your other customers how little they paid you."

Marginal pricing will work only when your customers *can't* (don't read that as "don't" or "probably won't"; the word is "can't") talk to each other. Because I'll assure you that if they *can* talk to each other, *they will.* Your federal and state governments make it illegal for vendors to fix prices, but they encourage buyers to compare prices. If your customers can talk, be assured they will.

The theory of marginal pricing or incremental pricing is a great academic concept. There's only one thing that the economists forget to tell you when they advise you to do it. Your customers are likely to compare notes. And when they do, your price-buyer (to whom you cut this great deal) will tell your other customers about the deal and, in the bargain, ends up training your other customers to go after the same, lower price. Let me give you an example or two.

Purchasing agents talk to each other. Buyers talk to each other. Owners of companies talk to each other. But guess what? They almost always talk to people in *THEIR industry*. Contractors talk to contractors, manufacturers talk to manufacturers and retailers talk to retailers. But, even more specifically, retailers in the clothing industry talk to retailers in the clothing industry, and people who manufacture concrete blocks talk to people who manufacture concrete blocks.

Your customers almost assuredly will talk to your other customers -- and it only takes *one* contact for the word to get out. Let's say you sell electrical supplies and equipment, and you sell to 27 electrical contractors in your territory. But let's say you're not selling to the other 49 electrical contractors in your territory. So, to "get your foot in the door" with a new customer, you cut your price.

You are going to slit your throat if you do that. You know what's going to happen? If you sell to this new account for $18, and you've been selling to your other accounts for $20, you can jolly well bet that, sooner or later, that new customer is going to talk to a buyer from one of your older accounts. And you know what they'll say. They'll start talking about business. And the new account guy will say to the old account guy, "Hey, you buy from those yo-yos?"

"Yeah, sure do."

"What do you pay for (copper, outlets, switches, etc.)?"

"We pay $20. What do you pay?"

"Well, you better learn how to buy. I'm only paying $18."

"The hell, you say!"

"Yep, you better learn something about buying."

"You can't be buying those for $18."

"Am too, am too! In fact I will send you a fax copy of the invoice on my last order from them, along with a copy of the cancelled check to go with it."

And the word will spread from there to all your old accounts. Now what have you just taught the old accounts? You've taught them to come and ask you for what price? $18? No, they don't want $18. They want $16 to compensate for having been taken advantage of in the past, right? I've seen that happen. Remember, purchasing agents talk, owners of companies talk, customers talk. They get together, they have conventions. And even when people change jobs or lose jobs, they will seldom change industries. They just change companies. And they're going to remember what they were paying over there. Never forget, you end up *training* your customer to beat you up on price.

- *THEY SAY, WE DON'T CARE ABOUT QUALITY, SERVICE, DELIVERY. IT DOESN'T MAKE ANY DIFFERENCE. PRICE IS ALL THAT'S IMPORTANT."*

When this happens tell your customer, "Okay! We'll ship it to you in four years." But then they'll say, "Oh no, no, we have to have it next Thursday." Then say, "So, you do care about delivery," to which they will reply, "Well, yeah, but quality's not important." Say, "OK, then we'll ship you the rejects." But then they'll say, "No, no, it's got to be top stuff."

When your customer says they don't care about quality, service or delivery, they are really trying to negate your competitive edge. They'll say, "We don't care about this, we don't care about that, all we care about is the price." But they are saying that in hopes they can get you to cut your price and still get better quality, service and delivery from you. If you push them, every time they'll say, "No, we have to have it by_____," or, "We can't take seconds."

- *THEY CHANGE THE QUALITY, SERVICE, DELIVERY ONCE YOU HAVE STRUCK YOUR DEAL.*

Here's the way this one works: On a scale of 1 to 10, they say, "We have to have top quality, top service, immediate delivery. In short, we want a 10."

Of course, you'll say, "Then the price is a 10. You want a 10, the price is a 10." But they will say, "No, no, no. The price has got to be 5."

Now wait a minute -- why is it *always* and *only* your *price* that's negotiable? Why isn't anything other than your price negotiable?

One thing you must remember is that *everything* is negotiable, not just price. Keeping that in mind you may end up driving a hard bargain -- and strike a deal. But that is not the end of it. For what this trick amounts to is that *after* you have struck a deal -- say you promise an "8" on quality, service and delivery, at a price of "8", then they *raise* the quality, service, and delivery back to a "10" *after* the deal is struck. And they almost always do it the same way -- they call you and you hear this silly, nervous laugh and it goes as follows, "Hee, hee, um, uh, guess what? You know that stuff we set up for three weeks delivery? Well, hee, hee, my boss said we've got to have that stuff by Thursday. That won't be any problem, will it?"

If you say, "Oh, that won't be any problem," you are crazy! Because what they are trying to do is trick you into a Thursday delivery -- at the three week delivery price! That is, they want your ability to deliver -- at your competitor's price!!

How do you handle this? If you are smart, what you say is, "Oh, yeah, I think we can do that for you, *but let me find my water-cooled calculator* so we can figure out what it's going to cost you *extra.*"

On these deals you must always use your water-cooled calculator. You can't use an electronic calculator because it will overheat. That's because any changes of this nature require the use of big, wide numbers and you have to keep hitting the "X" bar so many times that any conventional, high-tech calculator will just blow all its circuitry. The principle is this: If your customer ever wants to change *anything*, you must raise the price. That is true, whether he wants to change things up *or* down; whether he wants more *or* less. And if you don't believe that is done, look at what the oil and gas industry did in the United States. When we said we wanted lead in our gas, they said, "That will cost you extra." But when we said we *didn't* want lead in our gas anymore, they said, "That will cost you extra." And the oil and gas industry is only one example. Another example of this same phenomenon, used by shrewd business people, comes from the construction industry. In fact, the typical contractor has a word for it. He calls it a "change order". And he will tell you straight forward, "You bid the job close, but you make your money on the change order." Contractors *live* for change orders. Example: Let's say you're building yourself a little cottage out on the lake. And you're out there looking around while the walls are coming up. And you're in what is to be the master bathroom; but the closet looks a little dinky. You think, "Maybe we could move that one closet wall just a little ways; make the closet a little bigger."

So you explain the problem to the builder. And the first thing he'll say is, "Oh, my God." Then his eyes roll back up into his head, and then they will re-focus on you. Then he will say, "That's a load-bearing wall," to which you will say, "That's not a load-bearing wall, that's a closet wall. There's nothing below it. There's nothing above it. What do you mean, that's a load-bearing wall?"

To this he responds, "You don't understand. That *particular* wall that you want moved happens to be the *physical stress center* of the entire country! Oh my, if we have to move that wall....Oh, we're going to have to rip out everything we have already put in; we're going to have to tear out the foundation; we're going to have to push that mountain back about 40 feet...Oh my! We can't do it. Well, maybe we could, but we'll have to have an additional $200,000,000,000 to do it. Well, we'll see if we can do it for another $200 billion." Of course, this is an exaggeration, but you get the idea. Changes in the original deal automatically up the price.

Let me use a real example of how an association executive tried to pull this, "Let's change the quality, service, delivery at the original price," trick on me the other day. This gentleman called me up, wanting to know if I would be available to do a couple of days at his trade association convention. I could, and we booked the deal: two mornings, back to back. That was about June. Come December, about a month before the meeting, my phone rings. He identifies himself, and then he says, "Hee, hee, hee."

Immediately I think, "Here comes the change order. Get out the water-cooled calculator, change order coming in here."

He continues, "Hee, hee, hee, guess what? My Board has decided to do an afternoon session in addition to the two morning sessions at our convention."

I said, "That's great. *Who* are you going to get to do the afternoon session?" Well, he wondered aloud, could he maybe get *me* to do it?

You don't think I stuck it to him, do you? Well, I did. You're right. But only because I'm a consummate educator -- not because of greed. You see, I felt it was my moral duty to teach him about the hazards of a change order. It had nothing to do with my pecuniary gain. Hee, hee.

The honest truth is, had he been honest upfront about how much he wanted me to work, I might have agreed to do the deal at the same price for the two mornings and the afternoon as for the two mornings. Frankly, in my case, I'd rather work with the group then lay by the pool. But when he came back with that "hee, hee, hee", that was when I knew he was trying to sucker me out of a half day of work. So I used my water-cooled calculator on him. The thing is, you almost always know when they're working you, because it's always "hee, hee, hee". If they really made a mistake, screwed up, got themselves over a barrell, they don't say, "hee hee hee. My boss said..." They say, "Hey man, I'm bleeding to death. I'm hurting. I have to have this stuff by Thursday. I don't care what it's going to cost me; can you get it here?"

- *THIS IS THE TRICK WHERE, WHEN YOU ARE IN YOUR CUSTOMER'S OFFICE, THE BIG BOSS STOPS BY, INTERUPTS YOUR CONVERSATION AND SAYS INTIMIDATING THINGS LIKE, "ARE WE STILL BUYING FROM THESE GUYS?"*

Why do they do that? Well, with an inexperienced sales type, if someone important says, "I thought we decided to quit buying from these guys," the sales rep will often panic and think, "My God, I'm about to get thrown out of here."

You think that's not planned? You think that's not intimidation? You think they don't orchestrate that? The whole purpose behind this trick is to scare the sales rep who's never been through it before. By saying, "I thought we decided to quit buying from these guys," it is hoped that they can scare the sales rep into thinking, "I better go to the lowest price I can think of or I'm going to get thrown right out in the snow." Don't fall for this. Remember, you didn't just happen to sneak through the system. If you're there, they are wanting to buy from you. And, now that they're working on you, hammering on you, beating on you, all they are really telling you is they *want* to buy from you -- but they want to see if they can get you to cut your price.

- *THEY BUY ON THEIR OWN TURF.*

This trick is psychological. Psychologically, they know that they can probably work you on this point. They can rig all the props. They can shape all the events. They can put the competitor's literature on their desk to show you that they are talking to your competition, too. They can do all kinds of things. If nothing else, even secretaries can be programmed to come in and bring them little notes saying such things as, "Mr. X, the salesman for (your competitor) called to ask if his appointment tomorrow is for 10:00 a.m. or 10:15 a.m." Or they say, "I just received a telephone call from (your competitor) and he says that his price on those (products like yours) is only...". There's all kinds of shenanigans like that which go on. Remember, some customers will go to great lengths to stampede you into cutting your prices.

- *THEY ASSERT YOU HAVE TO MEET CERTAIN REQUIREMENTS, SUCH AS, "WE CAN PAY ONLY X DOLLARS PER UNIT."*

This trick is just another variation of the stiff-arm. When they say, "My boss said that we have to do this for less than ($15) per unit. Now I don't care how you get to that price, but that's what it's got to be," they are just trying to get you to knuckle under. There is kind of a particular way in which they work this one. A common example is, let's say you're selling something that has three components: A, B and C. And you're asking $16 per unit. They say, "No, no, my boss said $15 per unit. If you can get it in there at that price -- the three of them adding up to $15 a unit -- we can do it. I don't care how you do it, but we can't pay any more than $15 a unit."

Often, when they do that, the next thing they'll say is, "You were asking $16. How'd you come up with the $16?"

If you fall for that question by answering it, you're in trouble. Because if you say, "We're figuring $5 on A, $6.50 on B, and $4.50 on C, and that's how we got our $16," they'll say, "Come on, surely there's some fat in there. How about A? Could you maybe get that down a little bit? How about $4.50?"

You say, "Well, I don't know. Maybe I could go $4.75. And over here, on B, I might be able to get down to $6.25; but C, $4.50, that's the best I can do on C. So still it's got to be $15.50."

So you are hoping they will pay the $15.50. Boy, are you naive! The dumbest thing you can do is itemize your cost build-up; because the minute you do that, you have said that the *real* fat is in Items A and B, but there is none in C.

You know what they will say then? It'll probably run as follows: "Tell you what. We'll buy C from you at $4.50, but we'll look for this other stuff from somebody else. We'll put it together ourselves." That's called "shooting yourself in the foot", or identifying where the fat is in your own pricing. Whenever they say, "We have to meet a certain price per unit," you *never* itemize any cost breakdown, or how you build your price. If you begin to itemize your price on units that go into the product, you will inevitably identify where the slack is to your customer. The principle is this: If you talk in terms of a package deal, then only have a package price.

- *THEY CRITICIZE YOUR QUALITY, SERVICE, AND DELIVERY.*
"You guys are terrible. You guys are always screwing up. We didn't get one completely satisfactory shipment from you last year. Etc., etc., etc...."

It is an interesting phenomenon how customers (who are price-buyers) can so accurately remember all the things that went wrong last year, the year before last, the year before that, and on and on. I know one sales rep who swears he had a customer who was 24-years-old, who could clearly remember when his company got screwed up by the sales reps' company in 1938. I think that's incredible -- that a 24-year-old purchasing agent can remember what happened over 50 years ago. And if there really was a problem, they will never let you hear the end of it.

The way you handle this problem is when they say, "Remember back in 1938 when you guys let me down?", you say, "Yeah, that's right (if it's true). We did. But you know what? It's now been over 50 years and we've not failed you since. And we aren't going to fail you for another 50 years." Never argue with them; never disagree with them (particularly if they said something that was true). But turn it around. Use it as your own tool. Say, "You're right, but since then, we've been perfect, haven't we? We've done this, and that, and our delivery has been outstanding, our service has been faultless, and you've never had a problem, etc." It's amazing the way they can criticize little things, but you can use these criticisms as an opportunity. And remember, the only reason they're criticizing you is to get you to chop your own price.

•   *THEY LIE ABOUT HOW MUCH THEY ARE GOING TO BUY.*
Now I know this next observation will be no suprise to some of you, but I still have to make it. Have you ever noticed that when they lie about how much they are going to buy, that they always lie on the high side?

When you have a customer who says, "We're going to buy 100,000 of these puppies," and the most they've bought in one year so far is 3000, you know something is up. Something BIG. Like this year, they're going to buy 100,000; they're going to get 35 times bigger in one year, right?

There are three ways to handle liars. One way, with the real four-flusher, is to do this: (Incidentally, I don't normally recommend this, but if you've got a bald-faced liar that you need to control, do it.) Say, "You need a quote on a hundred thousand, huh? Ohhhh. I'm so-o-o-o glad things are going so well for you. Tell you what, let me get out my order pad here and let me write that down. Hundred thousand units, right. Hummm. Boy, that is great. Tell you what, why don't you take this pen and sign this purchase order for a hundred thousand units and then I'll write in the price as soon as you sign it. And then, if you like the price, you've got me; and if you don't, just tear it up."

146

Your customer will probably say something to the effect of, "Well, I really wasn't thinking we'd order 100,000 right off. I mean, I really wasn't thinking we'd order... that is, that our initial order was going to be 100,000."

So then you ask "How much was it going to be? 5,000?"

"No."

"3,000?"

"Yes."

"Oh, well, then let me get out a different purchase order and we'll write down 3,000."

The foregoing dialogue, of course, is a bit contentious. That kind of talk *might* get you into trouble with some customers. But not with a price-buyer who is trying to take advantage of you. The only time you want to use the foregoing is with an absolute liar. But, there are a couple of other, better ways to play it which are smoother and less confrontational. For example, alternative A is when they say "100,000", you can say, "Great, let me write that down. Now our price, when you order 100,000 of these, is $10 per thousand. But I must warn you, that's only if you order 100,000 through the course of the year. You don't have to start with that quantity. You can order as little as 1,000 if you want to. But I must warn you, if you order less than 100,000 at a time, you have to pay for them according to this schedule: It's $20 per thousand when you order only 1000; if you order 5,000, it's $18 per thousand; if you order 25,000, I can get it to you at $16 per thousand, and if you order 50,000, you can have it for $13 per thousand. Now, the point is, this price of $10 a thousand is good for 100,000; but I have to bill you at these smaller quantity prices if you order smaller quantities. But, *if by the end of the year*, you've ordered 100,000 total units, what we'll do is *rebate to you* what you overpaid when you paid in these smaller quantity prices."

The advantage to the foregoing is: (1) they have to order 100,000 or no rebate is due, (2) even if they order 100,000 and they do get the rebate, you have the use of their money during that period of time, and (3) rather than rebate to them in cash, give them a rebate in the form of a credit memo against yet future purchases. In this way, you keep and get the use of their money, *and* you've got a locked-in sale toward the future when they spend off their rebate.

Alternative B, which isn't quite as good as Alternative A, is the same deal -- only a little different. They order a hundred thousand, the price is $10 and you charge the same for the smaller quantities as above. But then you tell them that once they have paid the sum of money they would have paid for 100,000 units (in this case $1,000,000) in total, that you will then ship them the remaining balance of the 100,000 units. Same deal, only not as good for you as Alternative A.

- ### THEY SAY YOU CAN USE THEIR NAME AS A REFERENCE TO OTHER, POTENTIAL CUSTOMERS.

Of course you can. You can disclose your customer list if you want to. But why should you cut your price because you can use their name? You can use their name anyway. Unless you signed a contract saying that you would *not* disclose them as a customer, why can't you use their name? If I tell you I sell my services to XYZ Corporation, and if that isn't a lie, why can't I tell my prospect that -- unless I agreed with XYZ Corporation that I would *not* disclose it? When they tell you "you can use our name," of course you can. But you don't have to cut the price just because you can use their name.

- ### THEY KEEP STALLING, LOOKING FOR CONCESSIONS.

All studies I've ever read show that the longer a buyer drags out a purchase decision, the greater the pressure on the seller to make an additional concession, either on price or some kind of benefit such as improved delivery, quality or service.

Remember, time pressure is virtually always greater on the *seller* than on the *buyer*. Consequently, when the buyer starts dragging out negotiations and then dragging it out some more, they are trying to stampede you into hustling to close the sale. If you do that, you will almost assuredly make unwise and overly generous concessions. Don't do that!! Remember, time pressure is virtually always the greatest on the seller *until* the buyer has used up his slack. Then time pressure flip-flops and is far greater on the buyer. Don't let yourself get stampeded and get in a hurry to close. Be patient. Let them burn their candle.

Ultimately they will have to order and when they feel that pressure, they won't be so demanding.

- *THEY INSIST THAT THE USER -- THE PEOPLE OUT IN THE SHOP, IN THE OFFICE OR IN THE FIELD THAT USE YOUR PRODUCT -- DON'T SEE ANY DIFFERENCE IN YOUR PRODUCTS FROM OTHER'S PRODUCTS.*

When they say that the "users" don't see any difference between your product and your competitor's product, that is your open invitation to do back-door selling. When they say that, you say, "You mean the guys out in the field don't see why we are superior? I can't believe that. Would you mind if I go talk to those guys?"

When they tell you that "the guys that are using that stuff say yours is no better than anybody else's," they're pointing the finger at a decision maker or someone who influences decisions about what to buy. You *sell* to decision makers and people who influence decision makers, not people who handle paperwork with no decision making authority. Pursue your opportunity to talk to "those guys" that say you aren't any better than anyone else.

- *THEY DO THEIR HOMEWORK AND THEY KNOW ABOUT PROBLEMS YOUR COMPANY IS HAVING.*

When they use this trick they are trying to scuttle your confidence by kicking dirt in your face. But a lot of times, they are on a fishing expedition and are trying to get you to rat on yourself. For example, if they are fishing, they can't be precise. There is a big difference between these two statements: (1) "I hear you are having problems," and (2) "I hear you are having problems delivering those Ocotol units out of Philadelphia on time because of the breakdown in your supply of Phramis bands."

If they are *specific* about your problems, they know. But if they only refer to "problems", then they are fishing. Don't fall for a fishing trick.

Now, if it's true that you have problems, and they obviously know the specifics, you need to acknowledge it -- but don't let them beat you up. Hopefully, you have the problem covered, and you can say, "Yeah, we do, but don't worry about it because your stuff isn't coming from the Philadelphia warehouse. It's coming from the warehouse in Atlanta." Hopefully you've got a good answer if they have done their homework. But don't air your company's dirty laundry by saying such things as, "Gosh, how did you know about the problems with the Phramis bands," when all they said is that they *heard* you were having *problems*.

- **THEY APPEAR BUSY AND CAN'T GIVE YOU TIME TO SELL, THEREBY FORCING YOU TO JUST STATE YOUR PRICE.**

Here, again, they're trying to get you to stab yourself in the heart. They say, "Hey, look, I don't have time to listen to all this garbage about quality, service, and delivery. Just give me your price."

Now they might be telling you the truth, but if they don't have time to listen, you can't sell. And if they are a genuine, valuable prospect, they want to hear about what you have to offer. So simply test this statement by offering to come back *when they do have time*. You say, "Oh, I didn't realize this was an inopportune time for me to call. Tell you what. When will you have some time? How about tomorrow afternoon or could I come back on Monday morning? Let's make an appointment."

When they say, "I don't have time to listen," what they are really trying to do is stampede you into cutting your price by preventing you from selling your quality, service and delivery . If they are successful at this, then they have been able to put all emphasis on price *because you let them.*

The way for you to parry this thrust is to make an appointment for when they will have time. If they won't make an appointment, they aren't going to buy from you, anyway -- at least not at a profitable price.

- **THEY USE THE OLD "ROCK BOTTOM PRICE" PLOY.**

They say, "Look, I don't have time to make an appointment on Friday or on Monday. In fact, I'm leaving here in 10 minutes, I'm going to go on vacation and I won't be back for six years, so I've got to have your absolute rock bottom price if you want in this game. If you want this order, you better give me your best price, and you better give it to me *right now* because this whole decision is based on price."

When they do this to you, you go for the close with the slam-dunk. You go for the sale. You need to understand the logic of this. If they know all about your quality, service, and delivery; your competitor's quality, service and delivery; and they know your competitor's price; and the only thing they don't know is your price; and all they need to know is your price -- and nothing but your price; and any purchase decision is made on price -- and price alone; then they must be *ready to sign* when they get your price. So you simply reply, "Great, tell you what. Get your pen out. Get ready to sign your purchase order because I'm going to give you my best price. But this price that I'm going to give you is only going to be good for *two minutes.* I want you to know that before I give you this price." (If that is too tough for you to do, just say, "Hey, great, that means you can commit to the order right now if my price is the best price. Right?")

In this situation you must go for the close. The reason is because if they *know* everything, and their decision is strictly a price decision, you don't have a sale to lose, do you? If this decision is going to be made strictly on price, and if your price is too high, you were never in the game to begin with. You never had a prospective sale to lose. But you might *gain* a sale -- even if your price is *higher* than your competitors (if your prospect is willing to pay you a little more than your competitor and you can be convincing about the two-minute limit on the decision). Always ask, before committing your best price, if the customer is ready to buy *right now.*

Example: You're asking $18, the customer says your competition is asking $17. You think your customer is willing to pay you $.50 more than your competitor, but not $1. So now the decision is on you. If you want in this game, you have to give them your "best price". So test your price by first asking, if you give them your best price, *right now* (like they are demanding), can they *commit* right now? Then you can give them your best price, but it is only good for two minutes. Put the same pressure on them that they've put on you.

So let's say the customer then says, "Okay," and you say, "Okay! It's what I told you: $18.00." By doing this you have now initiated a price check.

Understand that when you give your "best price", you will force an answer of "yes" or "no". If the answer is "yes", write up the order. But if the answer is "no", take a walk. To be sure, the customer can now buy from your competitor at $17. Unless, of course, he/she was lying about your competitor's price (or was telling the truth *but* is not willing to pay you more than a $.50 premium over your competitor's price). He/she can still go talk to the other rep and say, "Hey, you know, you're going to have to get your price below $17 or I can't do business with you." And maybe your competitor will cut further, but maybe not. And if your competitor won't cut further, what happens if your customer comes back to you? *Your last price was too low!!*

If the customer comes back to you and says, "Well, tell you what. We talked it over and we can pay you $17.75," it has just been acknowledged that you are worth more, but maybe not a dollar more. Now you have the sale (at $17.75), or you can still test your $18.00. That is your choice. But remember, you will never know your price is high enough *until you lose a few sales.* You must test your price if you ever want to sell at top dollar. You do that by using the slam-dunk technique. Give your quote, but make it good for only *right now.* You have to learn to close a sale -- and you need the thrill of a slam-dunk. You can gain both of those by making a price check when they demand your best quote and they have to have it *right now.* And the best way to make a price check is with a price-buyer. Because if the customer buys at your "rock bottom/two-minute" price, you know your price is low relative to your competition. And if he/she says, "you lose", looks around, but then comes back with a counter-offer, you have at least learned that your price is competitive in the eyes of a price-buyer.

But what if the buyer says, "I can't commit right now -- your two-minute price isn't fair. In fact, you know I can't commit right now. I simply need your best price *right now* so I can bid on this job. We won't know if we can commit to buy from anybody until we get the contract." The solution to this ploy then is to get the customer to *commit to commit,* in writing. That is, ask for a *contingency contract,* one that states, "If we get that contract, you have the order at your (two-minute) price." Recognize, you don't have to hang a price out there for the customer to shop around for six months. You can bet that you would be expected to stick to your price when the company got the contract in six months even if your costs have gone up; but if it is known that your costs have gone down in the interim, you would be asked to offer a better deal. There simply is no requirement for you to commit to a price in the future, if they can't (won't) commit to buy it at that price in the future. It is always possible to *ommit to commit* (in writing) if they really can't commit now because of the contingency nature of the business. Never give a firm quote until your customer can commit. "When can you commit?" is a good question to ask in any selling situation, particularly when they try to stampede you into giving your absolutely best price, "RIGHT NOW."

- *THEY ACT UNREASONABLE AND DO CRAZY THINGS.*

This is one of my favorites. The reader will recall an earlier statement about some purchasing agents who got to talking about doing crazy things to make sales reps feel unsure of themselves. One purchasing agent told me, "You know what I like to do? I keep an old stack of papers on my desk, and when the sales reps give me their price, I say, 'What? You crazy?' and throw the paper up in the air. You'd be amazed at what a bunch of paper floating around in the air will do to terrify a sales rep."

Another buyer said, "You know what I do? I pick up my phone and throw it in the wastebasket. You can't break a phone. You ever try to break a phone?" Another said, "I always toss their business card in the wastebasket."

When your customer does something crazy, always remember that the more bizarre their behavior, the higher the probability they *have* to buy from you. Why are they going through these histrionics unless they have to buy from you or, at least, are under a lot of pressure to do so? We saw this acting crazy phenomenon in spades in *world class* negotiations. Many of you readers weren't even alive when this happened and you can finish the sentence. Remember, at the United Nations, when Nikita Kruschev started beating on the table with his shoes and said he would bury the United States? And he won with that strategy with world class negotiators.

Doing something crazy is a very strategic move for the customer if the sales rep is not aware of the tactic. Just be aware of it, and how to foil the tactic. If they do something really off-the-wall, the higher the probability they really need to -- or have to -- buy from you. Why else are they going to all this bother? So when they take and throw paper in the air (or throw the telephone in the wastebasket), how do you react? Totally nonplussed. When they throw a stack of paper in the air, you say, "Hey, that's great! I'm glad you did that; it looks like fun. But you know, I'm here to get your order. Why don't you sign this order, and then I'll help you pick up that paper ."

- ### THEY HIT YOU WITH TERMS TO THEIR ADVANTAGE AND USE FALSE BREAKING-OFF POINTS.

In this situation, they are both stiff-arming you and testing your resolve. They say, "Look, that's it! There's no point in talking about it. If you can't come in at $16, you're out in the cold."

When this happens, you always want to test them. You break away from the table (but leave the door open) with a statement like, "Well, we can't really do that, so I suppose I shouldn't waste any more of my time -- or yours for that matter. What say we both think it over and see how it goes for you with those other guys. I'll make it a point to call again in a few days (weeks, months) and see how things are going."

In negotiations, you have to learn to use false breaking-off points. And don't be afraid to walk because they will probably come back around. But remember, you've got to learn to lose a few sales if you want to sell at top dollar. You can't make every sale. Again, you will never know if your price is high enough until you lose a few sales. Remember market share, almost by definition, means you aren't making every sale. You should have some idea of the percentage of your sales calls, bids or quotes that you should close on. If you are meeting that closing ratio, you should be content -- especially if you're making money and the company's making money. Low price (or high price) is not the only reason anybody buys anything. And, remember too, even if the customer buys from your competitor, but will talk to you again, that is a clear signal that all is not well with the new vendor.

- ### SOMETIMES THEY'LL USE A SHILL TO NEGOTIATE WITH YOU.

This is just the purchasing agent's variation of the turnover game used by the police. One prospect starts hammering on you and hammers down your price until another one takes over and starts beating some more. The whole idea behind the turnover game is that the first one talks in big quantities ("We're going to buy 100,000. Give me your best price.") and negotiates you from $15 to $13. Then the next one takes over and says, "Well, now. We're talking about $13 and so on and so forth, and we want this and we want that," but conveniently forgets that the number is 100,000 units; instead the talk is about an order of 3,000.

The whole purpose behind the turnover game is so that they can *forget* what they want to and *remember* what they want to. And what they'll remember is your lowest price and other things they want to remember. What they'll forget is how much they're supposed to order.

Remember, the price of a product is not just the dollar value per unit, but the total agreement: the terms of payment, the freight, who (and where) it is shipped, who it's billed to, warranty coverage and commitment, any delivery charges, any changes in the contract, any specific volume of business. What they do in the old turnover game is they conveniently forget what it was that they didn't want to remember.

The only way for you to handle this trick is when they have a new player on the field, you go right back to your old price. And when they say, "But, Joe said you'd agreed to $13," you say, "Yeah, but he didn't buy then. Are you buying?" (Notice the set-up for the slam-dunk?) You come right back out with, "You buying? I'll give you the same deal he had, but he wasn't buying at that price and that deal. I'll give you that deal at those terms and quantities. But if you want to start talking different terms and quantities, we're going to have to go back to the beginning and start talking again about the terms of payment, who's going to pay the freight, where it is going to be delivered, how many job sites it's going to have to be delivered to, etc." You're just spring-loaded. You go right back to your original position when there is a new player on the field.

• *THEY ASK FOR THROW-INS.*

This trick is called nibbling. I always like nibbling myself, as a buyer, and the people that teach purchasing skills teach buyers to nibble. I'll never forget this one instructor who was teaching a group of purchasing agents and buyers. He said, "Let's suppose that *you* are buying *yourself* this new red Porsche convertible for $80,000. You've just negotiated the best deal you can on the price, so now you say to the sales rep, 'I'll buy, where do I sign?' But just as you go to sign, you pull the pen off the contract and you ask, 'Now this car will come with a full tank of gas, won't it?' "

What red-blooded sales rep has got courage enough at this point to say "No." ? What sales rep is going to queer the sale of this $80,000 Porsche over $8.00 worth of gas? Virtually none will. But you, as sales rep, better learn to handle this situation. If you are the salesperson, you've got to say, "No." Because if you don't say, "No," the buyer is going to own your family farm. If you say, "Aw, sure, I'll make sure it's filled myself before we deliver it," he will surely then say, "Great, great. Now, where was I? Oh, yeah," and he will go to sign the contract again, but then will *again* pull the pen off the pad and say, "Oh, yeah, one more thing. My wife wanted me to be sure to ask if we get free floor mats with the car? We will, won't we?" And you'll say, "Free floor mats. Yeah. Sure." And he'll say, "Great, I just wanted to be sure. Now, let's see, where was I; I was signing it." But then he'll say, "Oh, and my daughter wanted me to ask, will you wash and wax it once a week for the first year?" And you'll say, "Sure," and then he'll ask if you will throw in the dealership. And the last request is for your family farm and *then* he will actually sign the deal.

You have to say, *"NO."* It's not a question of *if* you say no; it's a question of *when.* A good nibbler is going to own your family farm if you don't say *"NO".*

The logic here is that when you say no, you've given him the very problem he thought he gave you. When you say, "No, it doesn't come with a full tank of gas," then he's got this problem: Is he going to queer the purchase of this $80,000 red Porsche convertible over $8 worth of gas? Come on now. JUST SAY NO. He is really committed to buying the car from you at this time. He's not going down the street over $8.00.

But what if you can't say no? Baby needs shoes; you need a sale today. You just *can't* say no. If you just can't say no, then use the slam-dunk. When he says, "Now, this will come with a full tank of gas, won't it?" you say, "Yes, but only if you can sign the contract right now." Translation: "Yeah, you get the gas, but don't even think floor mats. You try for the floor mats and you are going to lose the gas."

156

Another ploy is to make a demand of the customer. For example, a seminar participant told me that his wife was a buyer for some retail chain and she loved to nibble. He said they were out buying themselves a waterbed set for their bedroom at home and she got into nibbling. And just as she goes to sign the contract, she says to the sales rep, "Now, you will throw in a couple of pillows if we buy this waterbed set, won't you?" Without batting an eye, the sales rep looked her squarely in the face and said, "Yes, but only if we can have a photograph of you in the bed with the pillows that we can use for promotional purposes in the future." He said his wife's jaw dropped....and then she took her pen and signed the contract. He said he thinks that permanently broke her of nibbling.

Understand, if you can't -- just can't -- say no, then handle the nibble by saying, "Yes, but no more." "Yeah, I'll throw in the tank of gas, but only if you sign right now." Or make a demand of them. Also, remember that the first nibble is almost always the smallest nibble, thus the cheapest and least painful to concede. So learn to *ask for the order on the first nibble*. If you don't squash it at that time, they are going to go for your family farm.

- *THEY SAY, "WE COULD BUY AT ANY PRICE IF ONLY..." OR, "MY BOSS SAID WE COULD PAY ANYTHING IF YOU COULD ONLY GET IT HERE BY THURSDAY."*

How to handle this? Slam-dunk! Ask for the order. Because if you say, "Oh, yeah, we can get it by Thursday," then they will start hammering you on price again.

Never make a concession without asking for something (like the order). Don't say, "Sure, we can get it by Thursday." Instead try this response: "Let's suppose we could get it by Thursday, could you sign the contract right now?" Or better yet, say, "Let's suppose we could get it by Thursday, what are you willing to pay?" Force them to come up with a price or to acknowledge that you will have to ask for a higher price for this special request by them. Don't give away your competitive edge (which, in this case, is Thursday delivery). When they're talking to you, making demands, and they're saying, "Hey, my boss said we could pay anything if we can only get that by Thursday," you put a price on Thursday delivery. You say, "Let's suppose we can. What are you willing to pay?" or, "That will cost you X dollars." That clearly puts up, front and center, the fact that you are negotiating the value of *delivery on Thursday* to them (which is what they're really trying to buy and may be the real reason they know they will [must] buy from you).

- *THEY WALK OUT ON A DEAL OCCASIONALLY -- JUST TO "TEACH YOU".*

Once in a while a purchasing agent (buyer or customer) is going to take a walk just to "teach you". I've even seen them walk out on deals where the price they were walking *from* was a *lower* price than they were walking into, knowingly, to "teach you". "Teach you" from the standpoint of, "Look, I told you -- you have to do better and I'll prove it." Those companies who do this (pay more to your competitor) view this as an *investment* in beating you up on *future* prices.

You can (and will) lose some sales on those deals. They will go down the road and pay somebody else money to teach you that when they say, "You have to do better," they mean you have to do better.

In coping with this tactic, you have to remember two things: (1) It often costs them a lot of money to change vendors and (2) your statistics on how much business (market share) you have to gain if you cut price to sell something, which normally makes cutting price a really stupid thing to do.

You can't make every sale. And maybe you don't want every sale -- at least not to a price-buyer. Furthermore, frequently they'll counter your offer with an alternative (lower) price just to test you. And some of them, no matter what your price is, will adamantly tell you they can't pay that much or need a lower price.

Many people who study and teach buying and negotiations will tell their trainees to counter the offer --no matter what it is. You need to recognize that when somebody comes back with a smaller price, it doesn't mean that that's the most they're going to pay or can pay. And, again, when they come back with a lower price, you just test it by saying, "Well, that's interesting, but have you considered what you'll be losing if you don't buy from us? You're going to lose

PRICE AS A COMPETITIVE EDGE

Price Usually Means:

$/ Unit

+ Terms of Agreement

+ Terms of Payment

+ Freight

+ Who Shipped To

+ Who Billed To

+ Warranty

+ Delivery

+ Changes in the Contract

+ Specific Volume of Business

159

our quality; and you're going to lose our service, access to our spare parts, our knowledge and expertise, our complete line, etc., etc. " Don't give them a big guilt feeling -- just straight-forwardly say, "Hey, do you know what you'll be losing?" and run it right back around to the subject of your superior quality, service and delivery.

- *THEY NEGOTIATE TRIVIA.*

Again, this is another variation of nibbling. They start talking about who's going to put the gift wrap on it or the markings, or who should pay for the fax transmission or whatever the heck it might be. Handle it like nibbling because *now* the cost to you is *trivial* -- "If I could do that, could you commit to the order right now?"

- *THEY LEARN TO GET TOUGHER AT THE END OF NEGOTIATIONS.*

Any good negotiator or purchasing agent invariably will get tougher along toward the end of negotiations. Studies show that sales reps, in an effort to clinch a deal, will tend to make far more concessions toward the end of negotiations. The principle that emerges is that when you smell or sense you have a deal, quit making concessions because that's when you really are apt to shoot yourself in the foot. When your customers start to take tough stands, you should quit making concessions and use up (burn up) their time. Remember, at that point, when they've decided to buy and they start getting tough, their wick's burning in melted wax. They have probably wasted all their slack and now time pressure is beginning to be greater on them than on you.

- *THEY SAY, "WE NEED TO REDUCE TO ONLY TWO VENDORS. IF YOU WANT TO BE ONE OF THEM, YOU WILL HAVE TO CUT YOUR PRICE."*

This technique is known as whipsawing. Because if you say, "Well, all right, I can give you this price," what they'll do next is go to your competitor and say the same thing: "My boss said we have to cut to two vendors. These two have cut their price. If you want to be one of the two vendors, you have to be below them." And then they go to another vendor with the same line. And they just keep whipping all of you back and forth until finally somebody says, "I can't do it."

How do you handle this? When they say, "We have to reduce to two vendors and if you want to be one of them, you have to give us a better price," you come back with the old, reliable slam-dunk: "Could you commit if I gave you my best price right now -- or do you have to go shopping? I'll give you my best price, but it's only good for two minutes." You must put the same heat on them that they are putting on you.

But what if they trick you here by saying, "Yeah, I can buy right now" and then once you've given them your "best price", they say, "You lose," and then take your best price and shop it? No problem. Remember the *Principle of Shane*? If they "trick you" out of your best price and then go shop it, they are doing *research* for you -- checking your deal against every one of your competitors. Remember, if they come back, your last quote was too low (or why would they have come back?) Had they found a better deal, they simply would not have come back. This is asolutely true if they actually buy from your competitor and then come back to you.

- *THEY SAY, "I NEED A REASON TO CUT-OFF THIS LONG-TERM VENDOR. FOR ME TO DO SO, YOU MUST BE BELOW THEIR PRICE."*

This is just like the foregoing. If you say, "Okay, I'll do it," they'll go to their long-term vendor and say, "Hey, you know this upstart company? They're below your price. We'd like to keep you as a vendor, but if you want to remain our long-term vendor, you will have to be below the upstart's price." Again, they just whip you back and forth.

You handle this the same as above. You ask them to buy right now, and tell them your price is only going to be good for two minutes. Remember, even though they know your price, and they can say no and walk out (or throw you out), that if they come back (or let you in again) what that is telling you is *your last price was too low*. If they had found a better deal while shopping your "best price", they would have taken it.

161

• *THEY SIT WITH A BRIGHT LIGHT BEHIND THEM WHERE IT'S SHINING IN YOUR FACE AND YOU CAN'T SEE THEM VERY WELL -- OR YOU ARE SEATED, THE DRAPES ARE OPEN, AND THE SUN IS BLINDING YOU SO YOU CAN'T SEE THE FACE OF YOUR CUSTOMER.*

It is really useful to have visual feedback when selling in order to read the signals your customer is giving. Whenever your customer partially blinds you, you can't do this effectively -- but they can improve their efforts because they can see you better.

Whenever this happens, remember these two words: *acknowledgement and encroachment.* Acknowledgement is, "Oh, boy, that light's really blinding me." And encroachment is, "You don't mind if I pull these drapes, do you?" or, "You don't mind if I turn this light off, do you?" or, "You don't mind if I turn this lampshade, do you?"

The reason for acknowledgement is really to say, "Hey, I'm wise to your game." The reason for encroachment (turning the light off or pulling the drapes) is to say, "and I'm in charge."

You can't lose by using acknowledgement and enroachment. If they did it to you on purpose, you've got to say, "Hey, I'm wise to your game and I'm in charge." If they did it inadvertently, you can't make them mad by doing the same thing, can you? If they didn't *realize* that the sun was blinding you, and you say, "Hey, that sun's really blinding me. You don't mind if I pull the drapes," what are they going to say? "Oh, I'm sorry, here let me help you." If they didn't do it on purpose, they don't want the sun blinding you. They want you to be comfortable. But if they did do it on purpose, you scuttle their efforts by both acknowledging and encroaching. It can all be done politely, using the same words.

• *THEY SAY, "WE NEED A PROTOTYPE. LET'S GET SAMPLES IN HERE," OR, "LET'S GET A WORKING MODEL," OR, "LET'S GET SOME DRAWINGS IN HERE. WE'LL WORRY ABOUT THE PRICE THEN."*

This one has cost a lot of people a lot of money. If you are ever in the position where you are going to *give away* your ideas, on the chance that you *might* get a sale, you better learn to charge for your ideas. Many a customer has broken a small business by saying, "We don't know if you can make it. Why don't you give us a working prototype. Once you've proven you can do it, then we'll negotiate the price."

Whenever a customer says, "Why don't you give us a proposal (or design, or drawing, or prototype, or plan, or outline, or working model or sample) and we'll look it over," you've got to charge for it. I'll guarantee you, once they get your drawings, your ideas, or your working model, they will walk it down the street and give it to somebody else to bid on. You can bet a genuine price-buyer will take your ideas and run down the street to "El Cheapos" to see if they can't get "El Cheapos" to sell it to them at a lower price.

The way you learn to charge for your ideas (or prototype or drawing or proposal) is to say, "Yes, we'll be glad to build your prototype (or submit a proposal or give you our drawings), but we must warn you, we charge 'X' dollars for this developmental activity unless, of course, it is not going out for bid. In that case, of course, we copyright and register our drawings (designs, etc.) to be sure they are not expropriated by other people." You'd be surprised what a copyright bug will do to cut down thievery, especially by *large* corporations (their lawyers know their company has "deep pockets" and they don't want any legal hassles). Also, the prospect of being accused of theft might seriously slow down your overambitious executive (buyer) who thinks you are too stupid to protect your ideas. Do copyright your ideas -- all that is required is the copyright bug © on the first page, plus the date and the name of the copyright holder. Just keep the original document so you can prove it was your idea first.

If you are really timid, and feel you just can't say that you will have to copyright your ideas or get paid before putting them on the table to be stolen, then another way to say it is, "Hey, sure we'll be glad to submit those ideas. But I must warn you, we charge 'X' dollars for this . Of course, that price is *applied* to the purchase price if you do buy it from us. Otherwise, we'll have to be paid for our designs and our drawings because, as you know, they are very valuable." All it takes is guts enough to say, "Hey, this is valuable. You know it and I know it. We're going to charge you for it." Or, "We're going to charge you for it; but if you buy from us, it's applied to the purchase price." This second option, of course, takes any "sting" out of your asking to be paid -- if they're honest.

If they're not honest, and were planning on stealing your ideas, they're going to get indignant as hell and say something like: "Huh, what do you mean? If you can't trust us, why we just can't do business." If they react that way, you know you are dealing with the south-end-of-a-north-bound-horse. All they were trying to do was steal your ideas anyway, and there probably wasn't any sale for you to lose in the first place. Just walk away from it or say, "Well, we can't give away our ideas, but we would be glad to bid on the other guy's drawings (proposal, etc.)." If they say you can't bid on *theirs*, ask why *they* can bid on *yours*? If they say you can't bid on theirs unless you submit yours, again tell them you will submit yours -- for a price. Or you will submit yours next time and you'll submit yours first; but this time you will submit yours *after* they have submitted theirs because you don't see any need to participate in a contest for the best drawings or designs. Presumably they know what it is they want done and are only interested in bidding it out. In short, find out how badly they want your ideas. And remember the difference between professionals and amateurs: Pros get paid. If your ideas, designs and drawings are as good as you say they are, they deserve to be sold at a fair value. If your prospect says, "The others don't charge," always reply that this doesn't surprise you because you have "wondered how professional and/or competent their people are."

Admittedly, this is a game of strength. But that contest (of strength) should be won by you if your engineers, designers, etc. are as talented as you tell yourself. What you will often find if you test this is that you will be paid, and that your competitors never really put in a proposal, design, drawing, etc. Perhaps they weren't even asked to submit one because your customer knew you were the best and wanted *your company's* ideas -- they just wanted them for free. Ideas are very valuable; anybody can do the work. And if you don't think copyrights (and patent) laws aren't tough -- and enforced -- ask any author, artist, musician or advertising agency how it is they can supply ideas and still get paid for them. In fact, all an advertising agency has to sell is an idea!

- *THEY PLAY THE POWER GAME RELATIVE TO HOW THE FURNITURE IS ORGANIZED, WHERE TO SIT AND EVEN ON WHAT TO SIT.*

Situation: They ask you to sit down. But the only place for you to sit is the couch over in the corner a hundred miles or so from where your customer is sitting -- and you want him to see your samples. Or, you come in and sit down -- but your customer seems to be sitting on a throne. He probably is sitting on an elevated chair (it's called the Mussolini technique), [16] or he has cut two inches off the legs of the chair you're sitting on, so when you sit down on the chair and you look up, your nose is just looking over the top of the desk and you're holding your samples up over your head trying to show them. Or you are asked to sit down, but the only place to sit is over behind his potted plant.

How do you handle any of these tricks? Just remember those two words we mentioned earlier: *acknowledgement and encroachment*. If he has cut the legs off your chair just acknowledge it: "My, my, this chair is uncomfortable. You don't mind if I stand, do you?" Or, if you had strong pills for breakfast, you stand and look at the legs and say, "Look at that! Somebody shortened the legs on this chair. You don't mind if I stand, do you?" Then you encroach -- you make your pitch standing.

Whenever you feel that you are seated in a compromising location, position or what have you, I recommend that you just stand up and take command. Simply say, "Gee, this is really uncomfortable. Do you mind if I simply stand here and talk to you?" (You might even suggest that your back is bothering you.) In a way the customer has really kind of forced you to flip flop the situation because when you're standing there, unless your customer is really big, you're going to be taller no matter how short you are -- and the high ground is working for you. Again, if you're *real* strong, sit on the desk. After all, it's a power game. Understand it for what it is and play it. Remember, when they pull these tricks, you merely acknowledge the ploy and then you encroach back. If you let your customer walk on you, either you're not going to get a sale, or you're going to give away the product and get nowhere.

---

16 Mussolini used to sit on an elevated throne to intimidate people, and that 's why judges sit on benches. It's a military tactic; take the high ground.

- ### *THE POWER LUNCH GAME.*

This is a psychological game. They take you to a big, fancy lunch. Society has taught us that if someone takes us to lunch, we owe them something. Just play stupid, enjoy your lunch and never feel guilty -- or obligated to cut them a deal.

- ### *THEY HAVE YOUR COMPETITOR'S LITERATURE ON THEIR DESK SO YOU CAN SEE THAT THEY'RE ALSO TALKING TO THEM.*

Experienced sales reps love this one. For one thing, good sales reps love to read upside down. In fact, veteran sales reps often lose the ability to read right side up, but most can read an entire desk top upside down in three seconds and commit it to memory --from 20 feet away, in poor light, through bifocals.

Secondly, it again gives the sales rep the opportunity to *acknowledge* and *encroach.* You say, "Ah, I see you're talking to our competition. I'm so glad you've talked to them because now you know you want to buy from us because of our quality, service, and delivery." Then you just lay your literature right down on top of the competition's literature and keep on talking and selling. If you're *real* strong, you might even say, "I'm glad you've been talking to these guys because now you know that you want to buy from us. In fact, you won't even need this." So you pick up your competitor's literature and throw it in the wastebasket -- or put it in your briefcase and carry it out with you.

- ### *THEY TRY TO SPLIT UP YOUR SALES TEAM.*

If you use a sales team, they'll often say, "Hey, your compatriot said we can get that for $18." The only way to handle this tactic is to say, "You'll have to talk to my partner about that because I'm not authorized to say that."

Incidentally, if you are exposed to a lot of dividing and conquering, come into the electronic age and learn to use tape recorders. Tape record any conversations when your partner isn't there so he/she can review what was said, or at least the salient points. This divide and conquer technique can be devastating. You've seen it done in retail stores. A customer comes in; pulls a jacket off the rack with $150 marked on it and says to the clerk, "I was in here yesterday and they said I could have this for $130."

What are you going to do? Only thing you can do, other than sell it for $130 is get tough. You can say, "Oh, yeah? Who said that?"

"Why, the clerk."

"Oh, well, what was the clerk's name?"

"I don't remember."

"Well, was it a male or a female?"

The answer you might get at this point is, "Oh, they all look alike to me."

When they use this "somebody else said" ploy, you must keep pushing, because they will lie to you or they'll misrepresent some degree of what they heard. You've got to say, "Hey, we've got to get that sales person in here," or, "I'll have to check that with Jan." Otherwise, simply say, "I can't make that concession; you'll have to talk to her."

- *"WE PAY OUR BILLS ON TIME, EVERY TIME." "WE LISTEN TO YOUR IDEAS FULLY AND FAIRLY WHEN THEY HAVE MERIT." "WE PROVIDE FEEDBACK TO YOU IN REGARD TO THE SERVICEABILITY OF YOUR PRODUCT." "WE SHARE INFORMATION ON PRODUCTION SCHEDULE CHANGES AND INFORMATION ON NEW AND UPCOMING PRODUCTS." "WE DON'T DUMP UNNECESSARY RUSH ORDERS ON YOU," "WE WRING THE 'FAT' OUT AT OUR END." "WE ADAPT TO YOUR (THE VENDOR'S) ORDER/SHIPPING PROCEDURES." "WE TOLERATE -- AND DON'T EXAGGERATE -- OCCASIONAL PERFORMANCE LAPSES ON YOUR PART." "WE EDUCATE OURSELVES ABOUT YOUR PRODUCTS AND THE TECHNOLOGY ASSOCIATED WITH IT."*

When your customer starts bragging about what a great customer they are, remember this: You don't have to cut your price because *they have done what they said they were going to do and should do as a good customer!!*

When they say, for example, we pay our bills on time, every time, you say, "Yes, that's right and we really appreciate it, and it's *because* of that good record that we've been able to give you this favorable price (that I just quoted you)." Don't say, "Oh, yeah, we'll cut our price because you pay your bills on time (like you agreed to)." Just because they did what they *promised to do* doesn't mean you owe them a price-cut. The same goes for all the rest of their bragging about what a good customer they are. When they say "We give you feedback with respect to the serviceability of your product," you answer, "You bet, and *because* of that, we've been able to give you the kind of product, help and service that you need." And when they tell you, "We educate ourselves about your products and the technology associated with it," you respond, "Yeah, and you know we appreciate that, and *because* you've done that, we've been able to also do a good job for you." Don't go cutting your price just because they start telling you about what a great customer they happen to be. They are supposed to be a good customer, like you are supposed to be a good vendor. If they weren't a good customer, you couldn't sell to them or you'd have to charge an even higher price.

CHAPTER 14

HOW TO CLOSE A SALE
WHEN YOU'RE FACED BY
PRICE RESISTANCE

"When in doubt, raise your price."
Zachary Raphael

It is certain that you will get price resistance from some of your customers. This does not mean they will not buy from you, even when your price is higher than your competitors. But you must know how to contend with this pressure. There are no foolproof schemes for foiling every effort to get you to cut your price, but some of the following (which reflects heavily on much of the foregoing in this book) should give the reader ideas to reflect on, and actions to take, when getting resistance to his/her price.

• *KNOW YOUR COMPETITIVE EDGE AND USE IT.*
We talked about competitive edge in Chapters 3 and 4. Remember what your competitive edge is -- if it isn't price, it has to be quality, service, advertising, promotion, salesmanship or your ability to deliver. You need to know exactly which of these are your strong suits. If you've got the right quality stuff and your competitor doesn't, emphasize quality. But if service is your strength and your competitor has the same quality stuff, learn to sell service. Likewise, if delivery is the key, as it often is, learn to emphasize your ability to deliver.

• *SELL TO USERS AND DECISION MAKERS -- NOT THE PURCHASING AGENT.*

Talk to and sell to the people who *make* the decisions, not flunkies collecting brochures and prices. Not all people in purchasing jobs are flunkies, but a lot are. The job of purchasing or buying is often classified as a "brother-in-law" job. There is no point in talking to someone who is only collecting information.

Remember, too, that you must sell to people who influence decision makers. They may be the people that use the product, the people that run the plant, or the ones that own the place. Always look for power and influence in your customer's business. Analyze and study their purchasing procedures to get this information.

Finally, don't be afraid to do back-door selling. Just learn to be tactful and diplomatic in doing it. Never forget that you will not be given permission to do it, so you must do it discreetly after determining who makes and/or influences decisions in that customer's business.

• *USE THE FAB TECHNIQUE: THE FEATURES, ADVANTAGES, BENEFITS TECHNIQUE.*

People don't buy products on features, nor do they buy on advantages. They buy when they understand what the *benefits* are that they will receive from the use of the product (or service). I don't need a (feature) sharp drill. I don't need a (advantage) lightweight drill. I need a (benefit) hole in the wall and I don't want to have to work too hard to get it. The features and advantages of the product will help me gain the benefit I really want -- a hole in the wall obtained with speed and ease. It is always a good idea in facing price resistance (or at any time in selling) to emphasize how your products' features and advantages translate into benefits for your customer -- especially if your competitor's products don't have those features, advantages and benefits.

• *DO CLASSIFICATION SELLING.*

Remember, some items are more important to your customers than others. Jet fuel is far more important to the airlines than is ice for passengers' drinks. **A** items are more important than **C** items. Don't forget that the importance of price in making a purchase decision is, essentially, inversely related to how necessary the item is to the buyer. When the item is not very important to the buyer, more emphasis is placed on price in the purchase decision. But when the item is critical to the customer, price pales in importance.

• FEATURE ANY PRICE OBJECTIONS.

If somebody says, "Hey, your price is high," say, "Yes. You bet. Our price is high. In fact, let me tell you why it's high. It's because we provide you this quality and this service and this delivery," and so on and so forth. Never be ashamed of having a high price. Remember your high price makes a statement: *a statement that your product is better.* Tell your customer you are cheaper, and your customer will believe it in every sense of the word. Tell your customer you cost more and he'll wonder why. How do you get off charging more than your competitors? Tell me (sell me on) why I, or anyone, would pay you more money for this. Remember, the fact that your price is higher than your competitor's will trigger a "the hell you say" mentality, which will spawn the most receptive, responsive frame of mind in your customer.

• UNDERSTAND THE MAGIC SQUARE.

We discussed this in Chapter 13. If your customer *wants* a "10" in quality, service, and delivery, you have to get a "10" in price. And if they say the price has to be "P -1", you say they're going to get "QSD -1". They have to pay for what they're going to get. They want a "10", they pay a "10". That is just a question of conditioning in negotiations.

Don't ever hesitate! When your customer says we can only pay X dollars, tell them that then they can only get X amount in quality, service or delivery. By doing so you authenticate the correctness of your asking price. By suggesting they can only pay less if they receive less, you clearly establish the price of your product as a "10".

• USE TESTIMONIALS.

Those who sell at high prices know that one of the effective ways to do so is to be willing to tell your prospective customer or buyer who else buys from you. In fact, many sales experts will tell you that testimonial selling is, perhaps, the single most important tool to use in selling at a price higher than your competitors.

You really can't hurt yourself by telling your customer who your other customers are. Even when your customer is of a mind that, "If you sell to them, you can't sell to me," you won't hurt yourself because it is better that they learn up front that you sell to their competition *before* they buy from you. Otherwise, you may lose *both* of your customers. Customers respond well to knowing who else buys from you because most don't like to feel that they are, "the only ones dumb enough to buy from you at these prices." Testimonial selling overcomes this fear.

* ## USE THE "FEEL, FELT, FOUND" TECHNIQUE.

The "feel, felt, found" technique is, basically, a thought process. Your prospect says, "Hey, your price is high." You say, "Yes, I know how you *feel*. Our price *is* high. In fact, let me tell you why it is high. Others have *felt* it was high, too. In fact, we sell to (testimonials) Ford, we sell to Union Carbide, we sell to General Motors, we sell to IBM. They *felt* our price was high, too. But they do buy from us -- and at these prices. They do so because they have *found* that by paying our price and getting our (service) and our (delivery), that it is well worth it." By dropping names of customers (Ford, GM, Union Carbide, IBM) you are slipping in testimonials along with the feel, felt, found thought process. In fact, often your customers will actually ask you for testimonials. This helps them determine that other intelligent buyers and businesses feel your price is worth it.

* ## POINT OUT THE SERVICES THAT YOU PROVIDE TO THEM THAT COST MONEY.

One way to sell at a high price is to let your customers know what they get for that price. Ask them, "Hey, do you know that we do this for you?" A lot of times customers don't know what benefits may come to them by buying from you that they won't get from your competition. If you don't tell them, *nobody* is going to tell them for you *and* they aren't likely to figure it out by themselves. Never assume that your cuustomer knows anything substantive or esoteric about you, your company, your product or your service. Don't speak down to them, but do ascertain what they know and tell them what they should know that they don't.

* ## USE UNIQUE SELLING POINTS.

Learn to use unique selling points. Uniqueness sells. Differentiate your product. Anything that makes your product different from your competitor's can be construed as an advantage. Remember when 7-up was an uncola? Now, what is an uncola? I don't know, but they sure raised a lot of ruckus about it in their advertisements, and I understand it was a very successful campaign for them. More recently, we saw a similar strategy used in beer ads. Miller Beer said they were, "Draft beer in bottles and cans." Their evidence was that the beer was not pasteurized -- they said they were different. The principle is this: Anything you have that makes your product unusual or different can be used to get people to buy at higher prices. That is what makes the market for "collectables". But you better get out there and honk your horn about it, or nothing is going to happen. It is unlikely that your customers will figure it out all by themselves.

- *GET PERSONAL: TELL THE BUYER INSIDER INFORMATION.*

Sales people who use this technique find it very successful, because the buyer often thinks he is *avant garde* or somehow ahead of the pack. When you say, "Hey, confidentially, you order from us and you'll be way ahead. Why, next month we should have our new computer on-line and we're going to be able to do this for you, and that, and we'll be able to give you 24-hour order turn-around, or whatever...."

- *GET THE BUYER BEHOLDEN TO YOU.*

This technique is designed to get the customer to feel indebted to you. These are the special things, the thoughtful things, that you do for your customer. This is when you remember their comment that they, "just loved those chocolate chip cookies at that place in Springfield," and you just happened to be in Springfield and thought of them and bought this small box for them (assuming, of course, they can take such a token gift). These are the little, thoughtful things that you might do -- not bribes, but genuinely thoughtful things. Remember though, be sincere about these things. Programmed or "no brainer" things of this nature will always blow-up on you, sooner or later. And remember, the more business related or oriented the thoughtful action is, the better. Don't ever forget that people buy from people.

• *ASK THE BUYER WHAT YOU CAN DO FOR HIM OR HER.*

Most buyers will tell you that the sales rep never seems to care about the buyer's problems. They'll say that what most sales reps worry about is whether or not they're going to get a sale. To employ this sales technique you need to ask the customer: "What can we do for *you and your company?*" "How can we design things or do things to really help you with the problems that you are trying to solve, or the problems that your customers are addressing?" Sales people who show genuine concern will tell you that you will get a far more favorable response from otherwise indifferent customers if you really try to help them accomplish the things they want to do or overcome problems they are having.

• *CALL AT THE RIGHT TIME.*

Unless you are cold prospecting, don't ever "drop in" for a sales call. Always have a prearranged appointment or a set-up schedule. If you just drop in on your customer, the implication is that your customer doesn't have anything to do and can just drop everything and talk to you when you feel like showing up. Remember how you have felt about people who have just dropped in on you? It is an insult to anyone with a job if you think they can drop everything whenever you show up. Also, under the heading of "call at the right time", remember to always be on time for your appointment. If you must be late, call and say you will be late and ask if it is okay to come anyway, or should you make another appointment. Also, make them honor your appointment. If they don't see you on time, ask the secretary how much longer it will be before the buyer can see you and offer to make another appointment. Communicate to someone how busy you are because if the prospect feels you aren't busy, he'll feel you aren't selling much to anybody else and begin to wonder why he should buy from you if no one else is. Furthermore, don't be afraid to leave an appointment when you have been kept waiting too long. (I think more than 15 minutes is too long.) Make another appointment to come back; but leave. Remember, you are a very busy, successful sales rep with lots of customers to whom you sell a lot of product/service, and you can't sit on your duff for a half-hour wasting time. You've just got too many other customers to tend to.

Perhaps it is also valuable here to give a few words on deportment while you are in a reception area waiting (for no more than 15 minutes plus a few minutes of early arrival time). Be friendly; tell your joke; but otherwise be busy. Checking over the accuracy of your last order is *always* a positive thing to do. Don't read magazines (or comic books) and expect to be treated as a serious sales rep, and *never* say anything you wouldn't say to someone's face. (Remember, many reception areas have electronic and visual security systems that may record any and everything you say.)

• *DON'T BE LAZY, LETHARGIC.*

Selling takes energy. You have to work to sell, and don't ever forget it. Do what your customer requires (assuming it is reasonable). Product and services don't sell themselves. Be sure to return phone calls, follow up on leads, study call reports, analyze trends, etc.

• *LISTEN, PAY ATTENTION.*

You know this. You've heard this before. Many sales are lost because sales reps don't listen. There are legendary stories of lost sales because the sales rep didn't know what the customer wanted to buy. The sales rep has to listen to the customer, the customer's ideas, the customer's wants and desires, etc. Studies show that the typical sales rep who thinks he/she talks "half the time" is probably talking 75% to 90% of the time. A good sales rep really only talks a small percentage of the time (under half) in most sales situations. There are many good books written on the subject of being a good listener. This is an essential skill for any sales rep and I would recommend investigating the subject further.

SALES TECHNIQUES TO USE WITH A PRICE-BUYER

You're going to have some customers who think they're price-buyers, whether they are or not. I don't think there are that many genuine price-buyers out there, but there are certainly many customers that think they are. What are some of the things you can do to get their order, even though your prices are higher than your competitors?

• *KNOW YOUR BUYER'S NEEDS.*

If you really want to sell a price-buyer, you've got to do your homework. You've got to know what it is they want and need -- and it isn't just low price. We went through all those things relative to what the buyer needs and likes in Chapters 6 and 7. In brief, they need good supply and good delivery; they need reliable, predictable help in getting what they need; they need good services and no excuses. Selling a price-buyer also requires knowing, from an esoteric standpoint, what it is they need and want. Again, you have to do your homework to learn these things. However, if you do, you are often able to face down the buyer that says, "I can get the same stuff down the street," because you know full well that while he can get similar stuff, or perhaps the identical stuff from that competitor, he really isn't going to have his needs satisfied unless he buys from you.

- *NEVER ARGUE WITH A CUSTOMER.*

When a customer says anything wrong or bad about you, your company or your product, don't argue. You are not going to win those kinds of arguments. Instead, learn to do this: Agree with anything that is said if it is correct and try to take control over the situation at that point. A lot of purchasing people that really study how to be tough as a purchaser are told to complain because complaining makes sales people nervous. That is why a lot of customers criticize your company, your product, your service, the last order, and on and on. What you've got to learn is that when the customer is saying things about you, your company or your product, it's often just to scare you into thinking you are about to lose the account. The object is to instill a fear which will cause you to cut your price as low as you can go, as quick as you can.

The best way to handle this is to use a technique called "fogging" -- i.e., be essentially noncommittal and don't resist or argue. But when he says, "Of course, you guys did do okay on this," or, "Well, one thing about it, at least you got it here on time," that's the time to try to take over and say, "Yes, as a matter of fact, I wanted to point out to you that one of the things that we do for you is that we've always had on-time, reliable delivery. And let me point out another thing...." At this point, you take over the conversation.

- *EXPLAIN TO YOUR CUSTOMER WHY OTHER CUSTOMERS BUY FROM YOU AT THAT PRICE.*

When a customer says, "Hey, man, your price is too high," you might come back with: "Of course, we're 20% higher than those guys. And I'm real proud of it. In fact, let me tell you why I'm very proud of being 20% higher...." You may want to take that a step further, for example, by coming back with, "We're higher, you bet. But you know, we sell an awful lot of this and we sell it to an awful lot of people. Why, we sell to this customer and that customer, and we sell to these guys, too. " (As pointed out above, it doesn't hurt to do a little name dropping here and let them know who your other customers are. It's the equivalent of using references and is a *very* effective technique. If, in fact, you can tell them that you're selling to one of their competitors, that might be the best reference that you can give them.)

When you use this tactic, it is good to embellish on why those other customers buy from you. For example, you can say, "Well, you know, we sell to this company and we sell to that company. They buy from us because they have found that our delivery is so reliable..., or that our service is indispensible to them..., or that our inventory of spare parts has saved them countless times in emergencies...," or whatever it is that you feel is your real competitive edge. In short, it's a good idea to tell your customer why your other customers buy from you because the honest truth is that this company will probably want to be buying from you for the same reasons.

- *EMPHASIZE HOW THE PRODUCT WILL HELP THE USER OF THE PRODUCT.*

If you know enough about your product and how it's used by the people who actually work with your product (who are probably not the purchasing agent or the buyer that you're talking to), you should be able to explain to that buyer (very carefully, knowledgeably, comfortably and credibly) why it is that the people who use this stuff prefer your product or service. You should be able to say something such as, "Your people out there in the shop will really prefer using our stuff. Let me tell you why. They have found that our stuff is better for... [whatever reason].

Always remember that if you've got customers who are telling you that "your price is too high" and that they "can get it cheaper from someone else," always ask yourself this question: Why is he talking to me? If any significant amount of time is spent explaining to you that they can get it cheaper elsewhere and why the company would prefer to get it cheaper from your competitor, after a while you'd think they would run you off because you are just wasting their time. But, if they don't run you off, they're clearly *signaling* to you that they really prefer to buy it from you, maybe have to buy it from you, or can't *really* get it (on time) from your competitor. In other words, they are simply trying to figure out some

177

way to get you to crack, knuckle under and cut *your* price a little more before they give you the order.

- *EXPLAIN THE ECONOMICS OF PRICE AND SAY, "WE NEED A FAR LARGER ORDER BEFORE I CAN JUSTIFY OR WARRANT THAT KIND OF A PRICE."*

Often there are economies to be realized with large orders versus small orders. If a customer really needs a lower price, maybe he's going to have to buy two year's quantity from you at one time. Explain to him, "We can give you a larger quantity price, but frankly you'd have to commit to (so many) units in order to do that. A few of words of caution if you use this technique: (A) Remember the quantities needed to offset a price cut (see Chapter 8). (B) Be certain you'll get paid. (C) Write a non-cancellable, non-postponable order, i.e., make sure you will get paid.

- *ASK YOURSELF WHY YOU (AND YOUR COMPANY) HAVE EVER SWITCHED A VENDOR. IT'S RARELY BECAUSE OF PRICE.*

Why do people switch vendors? Why do companies switch vendors? The most common reason (over 70% of the time) is screwed-up delivery. Very few companies drop vendors because their prices are too high. Thus, if you have a customer who is spending a good deal of professional time talking to you, it's probably because the current vendor is not meeting the company's needs (even though it is indicated that they are "very happy" with the current vendor). If a buyer is willing to spend time talking to you, it is probably a signal that the company has a delivery problem, a quality problem or a service problem with the current vendor. Try to ascertain what that problem is and then sell your company's ability to eliminate that problem for your prospect. This point is *especially critical* if your prospect is experiencing any form of delivery problem with the current vendor. If that is the case, it's imperative that they find another source. The buyer (and the company) may find that by trying your company, they'll have no reason to go back to the old vendor even though they are paying you more money.

- *DON'T INVITE PRICE COMPARISON.*

A lot of sales reps make the mistake of saying, "We're the best bargain, even though we're higher priced." Such a statement invites a comparison and you are like the old matador out there waving a red flag at the bull. If you communicate that you think your price is the most favorable, price-wise, you trigger the mentality of, "Oh, yeah! Well, I'm going to go out there and find somebody that's got a better price." Sometimes it's how you say things and the words you use, rather than exactly what you said. Saying, "I think we're the best value," is far different than saying, "We've really got the best price if you figure it out." If you tell somebody you've got the best *value* (in contrast to *price*), you convey a value judgment which is harder to go out and prove. But if you say you have the best price, a lot of people are hard-headed enough to want to prove you wrong if they get the chance, and you may trigger your customer into shopping around.

- ## *LEARN TO USE STOPPERS.*

What are stoppers? Those are things you might say or do that stop customers from thinking they can get yet a better price. Research shows that a lot of buyers or customers will keep beating you up on price until they sense that you're really no longer negotiable. Thus, the earlier in the game you can convince them that there isn't any more to gain by trying to get you to cut your price, the sooner they will quit hasseling you, and you may very well get the order at a higher price because of it. Here are some examples of stoppers.

I Can't Do Any Better Than This (Be Ready to Walk Out).
One thing a sales rep can say is, "I can't do any better than this. I've already given you my best price." But you've got to be convincing and say it with finality. Using the past tense is helpful in achieving this, particularly if you're in a negotiable deal. A second thing you might do is give the clear appearance that you're ready to walk out. If you're a good actor you can say, "You know, I've already given you the best price I can. I suppose I may as well put my stuff in my briefcase and..." prepare to leave. Presumably, they get the idea that they've got you just as low as you're going to go.

Do You Know What You'll Be Losing?
Another stopper is a really firm statement (question) to the effect of, "You know what you're going to be losing if you don't buy from us? Do you realize you're not going to get our...(backup of spare parts, trained people, our repair facilities, our overnight delivery...etc., etc.)?" Make them start thinking in terms that if they don't sign that contract, they are in trouble and are going to lose something far

more important than price.

We Are Better.

An additional stopper is just a firm, self-assured statement to the customer, "Yes, I know we're 10% higher than those guys, but frankly we're better. And I've already explained to you why it is and how it is that I think we're better. But let me just review this with you one more time..."

Use The Non-Quote.

The non-quote is yet another tactic you can use as a stopper. The non-quote is a form of the false breaking-off point, if you will, but gives you the opportunity to keep your foot in the door and to test your price. You say, "I don't know how good we could really do, but you're obviously still negotiating with other people and rather than trying to finalize this now, maybe I ought to come again (next week) and see where things stand at that time." Then walk out without giving your "best quote". This technique assures that you will get a last look, especially with price-buyers who will always work to be sure they know everybody's "best price". And remember, if they spend some time seeing you next week, they are signalling that they are still very interested in buying from you. You must have the quality, service and delivery they need -- you are only negotiating price.

Use of the False Breaking-Off Point.

You can also take the false breaking-off point a step further. Again, this is a "pack your tent and get ready to go" strategy, but you say something to the effect of, "I really don't think this is getting anywhere and maybe we ought to break-off discussions for now. You might think this through some more and I need to, also. Maybe your situation will change; maybe ours will. Let's just break-off our discussion for now and I'll plan on giving you a call next week." Again, that's a dimension of the non-quote, but it even suggests the possibility that you've given up, and might not even call back next week. This tactic is, therefore, a stronger tactic than the non-quote with the same advantages.

I've Got to Get to Another Customer.

Another stopper is the technique of using the approach that you have to stop discussing things now because, "I've got another (hot) customer." This technique is a little bit like the slam-dunk. You say to the customer, "This is taking more time than I realized. I really do have another appointment that I've got to get to.

180

Tell you what. We're not making any headway here; maybe it would be better if I came back some other time." Again, it's another way to put some pressure on the customer, particularly if they're running out of time to get what the company needs: the quality product or service that he needs to be there *by a certain time*. This also effectively communicates that you do sell a lot of this stuff to others at this price.

We Are Pushing Capacity Now.
A very strong stopper to use is the line, "We're starting to push capacity this year and one of the things we really are quite proud of at our company is that when we promise a delivery date, we make that delivery date. Once we get our machine time booked up, we won't be able to sell this stuff to you at any price. We won't sell anything we can't deliver on time, and we are getting close to filling up our machine times." Using this line depends upon what you're selling and the nature of your business. But the emphasis is on the fact that you are not going to take any more pressure for a lower price because you are worried that you might not be able to deliver product on time.

Our Quality Requirements Will Limit What We Can Do.
One more stopper that is very similar to the foregoing is to use your quality requirements as a reason you might not be interested in writing an order, especially at a lower price. It runs the same way, with a slight deviation. The line is essentially this, "We pride ourselves in our quality control. Our quality requirements this year are really going to limit our growth. In the past years, we really tried to service everybody and we found it was very difficult. We're going to put a limit on our production capacity this year because we want to be absolutely sure that everything that goes out our door is going to be top quality."

Naturally you're going to use this quality line with somebody who is very concerned about quality type requirements, and whether or not they're going to get the right stuff in their hands at the right time. Again, it's the, "We might not be able to fit you in as a customer this year at any price, let alone the price you say you want, given the requirements that we're leveling upon ourselves to have absolutely perfect quality going out the door" strategy. You can do that either from a quality standpoint or from the standpoint of your production capacity, or both.

181

In using stoppers you must remember you are trying to convince purchasing people and buyers that you, the sales rep, are no longer negotiable. You put the pressure on them -- fish or cut bait.

- *MAKE SURE THAT YOUR CUSTOMER KNOWS THAT OTHER THINGS AREN'T EQUAL.*

Your customer is always going to tell you, "Other things are equal and I can get the same stuff down the street, only cheaper," or, "Those guys are just as good as you are -- they have the same quality, service and delivery." But you know, first off, that many times it's *not* the same stuff, it's just similar stuff. Secondly, even if it *is* the same stuff, they are not getting it from the same company. It's not the same company policies, it's not the same procedures and it's just not going to be the same. So again, always know why other things aren't equal, even though they say they are. Point out to them why your product is different and why buying from your company absolutely makes it different. Say to them that, "You may think that our company is just like that company, but we're really not. And these are some of the things that I think you should know about." Then you start enumerating those reasons why you're a better vendor, even if you're selling the same stuff. And, remember too (as we said in Chapter 5), if they are willing to waste very much of their time telling you they can get it cheaper, they probably can't get it cheaper; or if they can, don't want to or better not!

- *POINT OUT TO YOUR CUSTOMER, "THIS IS WHAT YOUR PEOPLE WANT."*

A good sales strategy to use on a price-buyer is to tell them, "This is what the people that use this stuff want. I've been talking to your engineering people and they say that they've really got to have these things. I realize that our price is higher, but I'm sure you realize that you pretty much get what you pay for. And I'm here to tell you that the reason our price is higher is because we're better. Let me tell you why we're better." Then you talk about why your product or service is better, whether that's quality or service or what-have-you.

CHAPTER 15

GENERAL GUIDELINES
ON HOW TO PRICE

*"The mechanics of running a
business are really not very
complicated when you get down to
essentials. You have to make some
stuff and sell it to somebody for
more than it costs you. That's
about all there is to it, except for a
few million details."*
John L. McCaffrey

It is always difficult to price any product. And it is literally true that most
business people are terrified of overpricing. Consequently, when they have any
doubts about their price, they almost always make the error on the low side. It's
not unlike someone approaching the edge of a cliff. Almost always they are so
terrified of going "off the deep end" that they will inevitably be
ultraconservative in their approach.

It is not easy to try to decide when your prices are too high or too low. Chapters
11 and 12 presented some of the indicators of overpricing and underpricing on

products and services. However, I would now like to discuss some philosophical guidelines on pricing. For example, there is always the basic question: Should we be a higher price competitor or should we be a lower price competitor?

Anyone who has read this book in its entirety to this point will know that my recommendation to any business or sales person is basically to be a higher price competitor. However, there are reasons that one might wish to be a lower price competitor. The strategy of being a lower price competitor, or at least being on the low side of the competitive arena, probably occurs when the following conditions and circumstances prevail.

- *YOUR PRODUCT (OR YOUR BUSINESS) IS IN A WELL-ESTABLISHED MARKET THAT HAS NOT SEEN MANY CHANGES.*

Some products and some markets simply become established and there are very few, if any, innovations which occur in those markets. It is very difficult in a very stable circumstance to be a higher price competitor. The primary reason for this, of course, is that everybody and their dog has the product or can do a comparable job or provide an identical service. When this happens, you are competing in a "me too" market and you'll have to get down with the rest of the crowd to sell anything.

- *YOU ARE IN A SITUATION OF MANY SIMILAR OR IDENTICAL PRODUCTS IN YOUR MARKET.*

When you cannot differentiate your product or your service from your competitor's product or service, it is difficult to establish and maintain higher prices than your competition. It certainly can and is done. In Chapter 3, where we talk about competitive edge, it is developed very clearly that even when someone is selling a commodity, you *can* sell at a higher price. But to do so you must be very good at selling your company's service and/or have unique talent in terms of the ability to deliver the product or service into the customer's hands at the right place and time.

Many business people, however, don't wish to be competing in terms of service and/or they can't think of any way to be any better than their competitors relative to the service that they provide their customer. When someone has this mind-set, almost of necessity, they'll have to be a lower price competitor.

- *YOU OWN THE MARKET.*

If you "own" the market, or have an exceptionally large share of the market, you may wish to price low. The usual reason given for this strategy is to keep other competitors out.

Such a tactic can be rather foolhardy for one particular reason: some people will enter a market no matter how dominant a given major player is in that field. So no one should ever be so secure because of their market share, as to feel they can keep all competitors out.

Another point which should be made is that pricing low to maintain market share results in having such low profit margins that the company is not earning an adequate return-on-investment. That ultimately will doom the company, even if they have 100% of market share. There are many circumstances at work here. One is the inability to replace capital equipment because of inflationary pressures in that business. A second problem is the possibility of technological change requiring investments that the company can't afford and, of course, a third possibility is something critical going wrong in that business which precludes the company from continuing to survive. For example, the evolution of a very strong union that extracts totally unreasonable wages can even put a dominant player out-of-business.

If one needs an example of how some business can have a dominant market share, but still end up going out-of-business, look at the small package delivery business in the United States. Back in the 1950s, the dominant player was Railway Express Agency. But they don't exist today and they haven't for a long time. Since then we have seen the emrgence of UPS, Federal Express, DHL, Emery Air Freight, etc.

- *IT DOESN'T COST MUCH TO SELL YOUR PRODUCT.*

Some products (and services) can be sold without major expense in advertising and promoting the product. Obviously, if you're selling a product that can simply be put on the street, and sales are virtually assured, you'll probably have to be a low price competitor because you can bet you'll have a lot of competition also putting the product on the street.

The contrasting side to this occurs when selling your product requires major expenditures in advertising and promotion. Perhaps one of the better examples of where one had better be high-priced because of the cost of promoting the products occurs in the cosmetics industry.

- ### *YOU GET A LOT OF HELP WITH THE ADVERTISING AND PROMOTION OF YOUR PRODUCTS.*

Some products and services are expensive to sell, but the people who sell them get a lot of help from the people who supply those products (or components of the products) to them. It is not unusual for manufacturers to provide advertising and promotion help to dealers/retailers of their product. It is also not unusual for major component manufacturers to participate in promotional costs for the sale of a manufacturer's product when that component supplier's product is brand identifiable in the final product.

For example, let's say someone is selling agricultural irrigation equipment, and part of this package of irrigation equipment is an engine which must power pumps to raise water out of the ground and push the water through the irrigation system. The maker of that engine may very well find that their brand name is obvious and ever-present on that engine installation, and they may find that it is very much to their advantage to help the manufacturer sell the system (which includes their engine).

The bottom line is the net impact on expenses of selling your product. If it is not expensive to sell your product, you can price low. Or, even though it is expensive to sell your product, if you get help with your expenses in selling that product, you can still price low.

- ### *THERE APPEARS TO BE A BASIC DEMAND FOR YOUR PRODUCT WHICH IS PROBABLY GOING TO SUSTAIN ITSELF FOR THE VERY DISTANT FUTURE.*

Some products (and services) by their very nature seem to have a perennial demand. For example, there will probably always be a need for hair salons of one form or another. While it is true that some hair styles change and the frequency that people receive haircuts waxes and wanes, there will probably always be people with hair and people who will want their hair cut or styled

186

after a certain period of time.

When one is in a competitive environment wherein they are selling a product or service that has an on-going demand, there is probably some argument to be "competitive" in one's price. But do keep one thing in mind: Being competitive tends to make you a loser rather than a winner, and in every product or service, there is almost always room for improvement in some area, i.e., a competitive edge.

- *YOU CAN SPIN-OUT ADDITIONAL BUSINESS OPPORTUNITIES BY SELLING ONE PRODUCT AT A LOW PRICE.*

A classic of selling something at a low price in order to make money from the business opportunities spun out of the sale is the old razor blade example. For all intents and purposes, give your customer the razor; and heal-up financially by selling the customer the blades.

This tactic is sometimes known as "buy-in/heal-up". Not only has it been done in the razor blade industry, but it has also been done in other areas, such as the copy machine business. Sell your copy machine at a relatively low price; but heal up on the sale of paper and/or toner or other products that can be sold as an add-on or spin-out from the sale of the basic product.

The trouble with this particular tactic, of course, is sometimes your customers get a bit unhappy about the deal. They realize that you're "gouging them" with your heal-up products. Consequently, it is not unusual to find your customers doing whatever they can -- to include legal action -- to preclude you from healing-up on them. Perhaps the more famous case of this was the old IBM card-sorters of yesteryear. The trick at the time was to give the customer a relatively good deal on a card-sorter, but then require the customer to buy all the cards that had to be used in the card-sorter from the manufacturer (IBM).

- *YOUR CUSTOMERS KNOW WHAT IT COSTS YOU TO PROVIDE YOUR PRODUCT OR SERVICE.*

If your customers have a pretty good idea of what it costs you to provide your product or service, they'll tend to be resentful of your making easy money on

187

them. Therefore, it may be politically astute to be "competitive" in such a market condition. But when you follow this particular guideline, you must remember that many of your customers don't want you to make *any* money on them. Consequently, no matter how generously low priced you are relative to your competitor, if you're making any kind of a profit, they may very well think that you're making too much money on them. And keep one other thought in mind -- appreciativeness is not a characteristic trait of a price-buyer. They figure that if your product was worth any more, you'd be charging for it anyway. Therefore, whatever (low) price you're charging, they will probably feel that's the best you can get for it or you would not be willing to sell to them at that (low) price.

Perhaps the foregoing guidelines provide some food for thought for when to price low. The reverse conditions would probably indicate when one would be better advised to be a higher priced competitor. These can be summarized as follows:

You should be a higher priced competitor when:

1. You're in a very dynamic, changing market place.
2. There's nobody like you or your product or service in the marketplace.
3. You're fighting for a very small market share but can identify a niche for your product or service.
4. It is very expensive to advertise or promote your product.
5. You can't get any financial help in advertising and promoting your product.
6. You're selling a product for which there is probably going to be a very short-term demand for that product or service.
7. There's no way you can spin-out any additional business by selling your product.
8. Your customers have no idea what it costs you to produce or provide your product or service to them.

WHEN TO PRICE HIGH AND WHEN TO PRICE LOW --
SOME SPECIFIC DECISION CRITERIA

As we've pointed out, it is very difficult to decide when to price high and/or when to price low. Obviously, one must be aware of competition. But as we have repeatedly asserted in this book, it is foolish to base your price strictly on a competitor's price. The competitor may be going broke, doesn't know what he's doing, or has so much money to lose that there's no way that you can remain viable and be "competitive" with a competitor's price.

Although it is always difficult to determine if you should be a low price or a high price competitor, the nature of market conditions can be a fairly good indicator of when one or another strategy makes more sense. The following observations are offered merely as a guideline to decision making from a competitive standpoint. Studying the various points should give the reader an idea of when pricing strategy should be high versus when it should be low.

• *MATURE MARKET VS. NEW OR DECLINING MARKET.*
You will probably want to price low if you are in a *mature* market. The reason is that mature markets seem to be full of people with "me too" type products. You can be assured when you have a very mature market, with many competitors in that market, everyone is going to "know" what the going price ought to be. You'll probably have to be in there with the rest of them to remain viable and have any decent volume of business. Hopefully, you're as effective as everybody else in keeping the costs of delivering your products or services low, thereby insuring your own margins.

Obviously, if you are in a *new* or *declining* market, you should price high. The reason to price high in a new market is that if you are one of few suppliers in that business you can probably get a higher price. If you're the only game in town, there should be no problem with pricing high. Short of not buying, your customer will have to buy from you. When you only have a few competitors, you still should be able to maintain profitable sales volume at relatively high margins.

In a declining market, of course, you're going to have to price high because you're not going to be selling very much. Any sale that you get will have to be profitable in and of itself.

- *INTENSIVE MARKET COVERAGE VS. SELECTIVE MARKET COVERAGE.*

You'll probably want to price low if you have intensive market coverage. If you're "everywhere," you'll probably find it strategically advantageous to pursue market share and, in an effort to maintain market share, you will probably want a lower competitive price. Again, of course, you'll have to maintain adequate gross margins to maintain profitability on your sales.

You'll want to price high if you have selective market coverage. If you only sell to left-handed plumbers on the 5th Tuesday of the month, you better be making a profit on every item that you sell.

- *LARGE MARKET SHARE VS. SMALL MARKET SHARE.*

You'll want to be a lower price competitor if you have a large market share. Part of this strategy, of course, is to keep competition out. The problem with this is that sometimes your competition's so dumb they keep coming in anyway.

The flip-flop, of course, is true. If you have a small market share, your need to make money will require that you be a higher price competitor.

- *LOW PROMOTIONAL COSTS VS. HIGH PROMOTIONAL COSTS.*

If your promotional costs are small, you'll probably want to be a low price competitor because you can afford to be a low price competitor. In contrast, if you've got to spend a fortune promoting your product (something we see in situations such as the cosmetics industry), you'll want to be higher priced because you'll need higher prices to cover your margin requirements.

Sometimes you'll find that your own vendors and suppliers will give you help with your promotional costs. If you get a lot of such help, it could be that you could still maintain a lower price posture. Contrariwise, of course, if you receive little or no promotional help, you'll have to price higher.

- *COMMODITY PRODUCTS VS. ESOTERIC/EXOTIC PRODUCTS.*

If you compete in a commodity situation, you'll probably have to be competitive in price. When everybody has one, they're all the same, and everybody knows what the price ought to be, you must be competitive or you're not going to sell very much unless there is a way (and you really are willing) to sell service and delivery. On the other hand, if you have a very unusual, esoteric or exotic product, you'll want to be a higher price competitor. People are very willing to pay for unusual, esoteric and exotic products. Also, if you have a proprietary product -- no one can make one quite like yours because of patent protection, brand identification or anything else that differentiates yours from someone else's -- you can get away with a higher price strategy relative to your competition.

- *MASS-PRODUCED PRODUCTS VS. CUSTOM-MADE PRODUCTS.*

If you're manufacturing a mass-produced product, you'll probably be a low price competitor. Long production runs and economies of scale can work to your advantage. However, if you're producing a custom-made product, each one is a little different, and there are no efficiencies or economies to be had from producing large quantities of your product, you'll want to be a higher price competitor.

- *CAPITAL INTENSIVE PRODUCTS VS. LABOR INTENSIVE PRODUCTS.*

Another criterion to consider in your pricing strategies concerns whether or not you are a capital intensive producer or a labor intensive producer. If you're fully automated, mass-produced and very capital intensive, you can probably figure on large, efficient production runs and be more price competitive. However, if you're making one-of-a-kind items that are very labor intensive, and it is very difficult to achieve any economies of scale or efficiencies from machinery and equipment, you'll want to be a higher price competitor.

- *SINGLE USE PRODUCT VS. MULTIPLE USE PRODUCT.*

The versatility of your product is another consideration in pricing. If your product can only be used for one thing and you've got competition, you need to be competitive with that competition. On the other hand, if your product is quite versatile and can be used for a multiplicity of things, you can probably get away with a higher price. An example of a single use product might be a paint brush. You can apply paint and other liquids with a paint brush. A multiple use product might be an air-compressor. You can certainly apply paint and other liquids with an air-compressor, but you can also run power tools, operate radio station turntables and inflate things with an air-compressor.

• *SHORT PRODUCT LIFE VS. LONG PRODUCT LIFE*

You should also consider the useful life of the product. If what you are selling has a short product life, being competitive is probably necessary because your customer will be using a lot of your product and will quickly see disadvantages if your price is a lot higher than your competition's. On the other hand, if your product has a long, useful product life, you can probably get away with being a higher price competitor because your customer will not be able to make quick comparisons as to the value of your product versus your competitor's product.

• *SLOW PRODUCT OBSOLESCENCE VS. FAST PRODUCT OBSOLESCENCE.*

Product obsolescence must also be considered. You can price lower if your product will not be obsoleted quickly. This is because you can spread any developmental costs over a longer product life. However, if there's a high degree of probability of product obsolescence, you need to get back all that you can during the short product life.

• *LOW SERVICE NEEDS VS. HIGH SERVICE NEEDS.*

If you have to provide few or no ancillary services with your product, you can probably be a lower price competitor. On the other hand, if you have to give all kinds of services with your product -- customer service, warranty work, training and instructions on how to use your product, etc. (particularly if you can't [won't] charge for such services) -- you should charge a very high price to cover all of the additional work.

- *SLOW TECHNOLOGICAL CHANGE VS. RAPID TECHNOLOGICAL CHANGE.*

If your product is seeing slow technological change or advancement, you can probably price low. This has the same reasoning as the preceeding point on product obsolescence. However, if your product is receiving rapid technological change and advancement, you'll have to price high.

- *SHORT DISTRIBUTION CHANNELS VS. LONG DISTRIBUTION CHANNELS.*

The cost of distribution must also be considered. If you have short channels of distribution that are very inexpensive, you can be a lower price competitor. However, if you have very long channels of distribution, and particularly if you have to go through several levels of distribution, you better charge a higher price.

- *FAST INVENTORY TURNOVER VS. SLOW INVENTORY TURNOVER.*

"Give me margin or give me turn." Many people feel that they can make their money on the turnover of the product. If you have fast inventory turnover, you can possibly make adequate money by selling a high volume at a low price. However, if you have very slow inventory turnover, charge a high price. But again, pay attention to the material in Chapter 8 concerning the volume requirements for price-cuts. Remember: *Turn* rhymes with *churn*, and it is possible to churn and make no money but work very hard. Profitability still comes to those who realize margins; it may or may not come to those who have high turnover.

- *PROSPECTS FOR LONG-TERM PROFITABILITY VS. SHORT- TERM PROFITABILITY.*

Your long-term perspective relative to profits may enter into whether you want to be a low or a high price competitor. If you have a long-term profit perspective and don't feel any obligation for near-term profits, you can probably be a low price competitor. But if you need (or simply require because of your own standards) short-term profitability, you'll probably want to be a higher price competitor and not worry about the long run. Of course, as one imminent scholar once said, "In the long run, we'll all be dead," so one must question the advisability of seeking long-term profitability at the expense of short-term profits.

- *LIKELIHOOD OF SPIN-OUT BUSINESS VS. ONE TIME SALE.*

If you're likely to create additional business from the sale of your product, you might want to be a lower price competitor. That is, if you feel that you can heal-up on the profitability from the additional spin-out sales on product B that you realize by selling product A at a low price, this tactic may pay off. On the other hand, if it's unlikely that you'll receive any additional business by selling product A, you'll probably want to be a higher price competitor because you're not going to make any money on any other sales.

- *LARGE MARKET POTENTIAL VS. SMALL MARKET POTENTIAL.*

The size of your potential market is also a consideration. If there is a very large market potential, you might think in terms of selling a high volume and be a lower price competitor. Certainly, if there is a very small market potential for your product, you'll want to be a higher price competitor. Again, don't forget the economies of pricing explained in Chapters 8 and 9.

- *INSIGNIFICANT CUSTOMER BENEFITS VS. SIGNIFICANT CUSTOMER BENEFITS.*

If your product provides insignificant benefits to your customer, you'll probably have to be a lower price competitor. People who don't receive significant benefits upon buying a product aren't very likely to pay a premium price. On the other hand, if your customer is apt to realize a very significant gain by buying your product, you'll want to be a higher price competitor. If your product changes somebody's total outlook on life or the quality of their life, you can bet they'll be willing to pay a high price for it.

- *INDUSTRIAL MARKET VS. HOUSEHOLD CONSUMER MARKET.*

Industrial buyers tend to be tougher in the market place than household consumers. If you're selling to trained, industrial purchasers, you'll probably have to be more "competitive" than if you're selling to an emotional buyer who has little or no training in purchasing, acquisition or procurement skills. But remember, industrial buyers really are less apt to be as price conscious as household consumers.

• *LIKELIHOOD OF FUTURE TIE-IN SALES VS. NO TIE-IN SALES.*

Sometimes you can lock a customer into future purchases. If you can do that, you can get away with a lower price. On the other hand, it may not be possible to tie people into future purchases. In those cases, you can't heal-up on future sales. There are, of course, certain legal ramifications for tie-in sales and one should be very aware of these before attempting to pursue this tactic.

• *NEED FOR LARGE PARTS INVENTORY VS. NO PARTS NEEDED.*

If your customers will be committed to a large parts inventory to keep your product functioning or operating, you might be able to get away with being a low price competitor by healing-up on the sale of parts for your customer's inventory. On the other hand, if your customer will not be committed to a large parts inventory, you're not going to have anything to heal-up on, so you had better charge a high price for your basic product.

• *HIGH LEVEL OF TRAINING REQUIRED FOR USE OF PRODUCT VS. MINIMAL TRAINING REQUIREMENTS.*

If your customer buys your product and, as a result, has to retrain employees to use your product -- and particularly if such retraining takes a lot of time -- you will probably want to be a low price competitor. The converse is likewise true. If, as a result of buying your product, your customer will not have to retrain employees to use your product, you can probably get away with a higher price. The basic point here revolves around the fact that it is very expensive to train people. If a lot of training or retraining is required to use your product, you have to give the customer a motive to try your product. But you can rely on the fact that if he switches to your product, and has spent the time to retrain employees, he will probably not switch again for a long period of time. Therefore, your lower price at getting your customer to use your product will perhaps enable you to heal-up with future sales because of the unlikelihood that your customer will switch to a competitor's product once they have started using yours.

- ### GENERIC PARTS REQUIREMENTS VS. SPECIALIZED PARTS REQUIREMENTS.

If your product requires parts that anybody can supply, you better charge a lower price because somebody will try to heal-up on your parts business. On the other hand, if your product requires parts that only you can supply (because of patent or production capabilities or whatever), you can get away with a higher price.

- ### EASE OF NEW PRODUCT ENTRENCHMENT VS. EASE OF PRODUCT DUPLICATION IN THE MARKET PLACE.

If you can get your new product entrenched in the market before it is copied by "me tooers", it's probably a worthwhile strategy to come in at a low price. On the other hand, if there's no way you can get entrenched before competition enters, you better come in at a higher price which will realize your margins.

- ### RAPID QUALITY ASSESSMENT VS. LENGTHY DETERMINATION OF QUALITY.

If the quality of your product is quickly tested (i.e., food), you will probably have to charge a lower price. If somebody can simply test the quality of your product by tasting it or feeling it, you can bet they'll switch quickly to somebody else's lower priced competitive product. On the other hand, if it takes a long time to test the quality of your product -- months, years, or even decades -- you can probably get away with a higher price. For example, something that takes a long time to test is housepaint. Even a poor paint ought to last 3 or 4 years, and a good paint maybe 10 or 15. If it's going to take your customer 3 or 4 years to decide whether or not your product is any good, in the near-term you ought to be able to get away with a higher price.

- ### LOW PRODUCT LIABILITY RISK VS. HIGH PRODUCT LIABILITY RISK.

Product liability must also be considered. If you have a very low product liability risk, you can probably get away with a lower price because of the lack of probability of expensive litigation and other margin-eroding activity concerning your business and your product. On the other hand, if there's a very high probability of product liability risk, lawsuit or litigation, you better charge a high price. One serious judgment against you could wipe out several years, or perhaps a lifetime, of work.

The foregoing considerations are only a guide to decision making activity. Any given factor probably will not determine whether or not you should pursue a low price or a high price competitive stance. However, if in reviewing the foregoing points, you determine that the bulk of the indicators of when you should price low apply to your product or service, certainly you would be more advised to be a lower price competitor. Conversely, if the bulk of them have to do with indicating that your product is in the higher price competitive bracket, you would probably be better advised pursuing a high price competitive stance, and rely on the other factors to help you sell your product and maintain the margins and profitability that your company should realize.

CHAPTER 16

SOME FINAL THOUGHTS
ON SELLING AT PRICES
HIGHER THAN
YOUR COMPETITORS

"Even if you're on the right track,
you'll get run over if you just sit
there."
Will Rodgers

There are many things you can do to sell at prices higher than your competitors. However, there are some things you can't do and figure you will be able to get the business from your customer at a high price. Most of these "can't do" items are things that sellers (vendors/suppliers) do which antagonize or inconvenience their customers. Let's take a look at some of these.

• *LATE DELIVERIES.*
You cannot have late deliveries. No one pays big bucks for excuses and your customer is not going to put up with late deliveries. If your customer orders it, he probably needs it, or has to have it. If you have late deliveries, it shows a lot of weakness in your company: your planning is bad, your scheduling is poor,

maybe your vendor relations are terrible or you have cash-flow problems. But the bottom line is that your customer can't count on you to get the product or service to him on time -- and that will mean grief and aggravation for him.

- ## *PARTIAL DELIVERIES.*

Your company had better not have a history of partial deliveries. Partial deliveries show the same problems as late deliveries. Your customer thinks, "Well, the guy's limping through so far, but one of these days he'll probably completely fail me and I'll be left high and dry without anything." Nobody likes to take partial deliveries, certainly not as a regular diet. It screws up receiving records and creates more paperwork for the customer. Why should they put up with your screw-ups, disorganization, etc.?

- ## *DESTRUCTIVE PRICING.*

You should not be guility of destructive pricing. What is meant by destructive pricing is when you quote someone a price (or you cut a deal) and then you start changing the price or deal. For example, you "lose" a large order and claim you didn't write it (at that price) or you tell your customer you, "couldn't possibly have sold it at that price." Your customer will get the idea that all you are trying to do is sucker them into giving you an order, and then you're going to try to raise the price after the order is placed and it's possibly too late for them to order from someone else.

- ## *CANCELLING OR DELAYING ORDERS.*

Another thing that some businesses do that cause loss of future sales is delaying or cancelling orders. If you tell a customer, "We can't honor these orders on time," you destroy your credibility and put your customer in a bind. Delaying or cancelling an order is guaranteed to cost you future sales because you become identified as an unreliable source.

- ## *REQUIRING "ADD-ONS" OR RENEGOTIATING ORDERS.*

Some sales people get into the (bad) habit of requiring extra orders -- i.e., they ask for "add-ons" in an effort to renegotiate orders. Again, your customers know what you're trying to do. You're trying to sucker them in with a low-ball quote and then trying to spool it up into bigger dollars. They will clearly see that you are misleading them and creating a lot of extra paperwork for them.

- *SUPPLYING DEFECTIVE PRODUCTS OR PARTS.*

Any parts, materials, or supplies that you put out that aren't right will cost you sales. Customers don't want to put up with shoddy materials. You not only directly cost them money by forcing them to re-do things or to inspect every piece before they use it, you also make them worry about your ability to control quality and give them good product in the future. Why should they buy from you at any price if that is their outlook toward you?

- *ASSERTING QUICK PAYMENT SCHEDULES.*

There's nothing wrong with giving a customer terms that will encourage quick payment. It's not unusual, for example, to give some kind of terms to your customer to expedite payment -- like 2-10, net 30. Those "deals" are okay and are clearly understood. But when you try to truly stampede payment schedules, it will tend to indicate that your company has cash-flow problems. This can cause your customers to wonder about whether or not you are really keeping up with your quality requirements, how things are going in your plant or your business, if you will be able to continue to give them the wonderful service you keep telling them that they should expect from you, etc.

- *SUBSTITUTING MATERIALS, PARTS OR SUPPLIES.*

When you start making substitutions of materials, parts or supplies, your customer wants to know about it. It may be critical to them, even though you think it's unimportant. If you substitute any kind of a material, ingredient or anything that goes into the making of a product or providing a service, you may very well create problems for them. Again, their usual reaction to this is that it shows that you're not really reputable to do business with -- not to mention that you may create very expensive legal, moral or ethical problems for them in dealing with their customers.

- *HIGH PERSONNEL TURNOVER.*

You may not think that your customer should care if you have high personnel turnover. Maybe they don't. But you should know that your personnel turnover can have a negative impact on their relationship and ability to work with you. Often the customer only knows the sales personnel they deal with in your company. But there may be times that they have contact with the customer service department, not to mention the accounting department and the credits and collections department. There is nothing more maddening than for a customer to have a good working relationship with an individual person in your accounting department, only to call and find out, "Mrs. So-and-So has quit and I don't know anything about it. She didn't tell me anything, so you've got to pay right now or we will cancel your order." The same thing can occur in your customer's relationships with your production, warehouse, shipping or other personnel. When these things happen, you are just provoking and aggravating your customer. That gives them reasons to start looking for other vendors, even though you may be more than competitive price-wise. This does not mean you can never replace an employee, but constant turnover can have a detrimental effect.

* *LABOR RELATIONS PROBLEMS.*

It's possible that even labor relations problems on the part of your company will create difficulties for you in selling at high prices. When a company has union problems, people start worrying about on-time delivery of correct quality products and services. In addition, they may even worry about sabotage, and they certainly will worry about predictability and reliability of your performance on their contracts.

* *A POOR REPUATION AS TO ETHICS AND INTEGRITY.*

Most people believe, "Where there's smoke, there's fire." If you, your company or your business have a relatively poor reputation when it comes to ethics and integrity, it's going to be very difficult for you to support a higher price stature. Just as your customers simply will not pay you big bucks for me-too quality, service and delivery, they absolutely will not pay you big bucks for an inferior, difficult or untrusting business relationship.

Hopefully, none of the above are in existence in your company. Sales reps should be aware of how their existence can harm the sale of products and services at high prices. If any of these negative aspects of selling do exist, you and/or your company must take steps to eliminate them if you expect to receive a high price. They are the reasons that customers are willing to leave a low price vendor who has problems of this nature and pay more to get product from someone else.

IN CONCLUSION, SOME BASIC GUIDELINES

No doubt about it, once in a while you're going to be faced by a price-cutting fool no matter what I write in this book. What are you to do when you have a competitor who is really hammering on your price? Keep these ideas in mind:

#1: *Never let the dumbest (or the fattest) guy in town set your price.*

Remember how much more volume you're going to need just to make the same profit dollars if you cut your price (See Chapter 8).

#2: *Determine how much, if any, your customer will benefit from any price reductions.*

There may be a problem of image if you cut the price of your product. If your product is associated with "cheap", you may rue the day you cut your price because you can hurt your product sales with too low a price.

#3: *Learn to resist the temptation to take action just for the sake of doing something.*

Cutting price usually will only get your competition to cut their price even further. It seldom gets you a lot more volume. This is especially true in a recessional period. Cutting price only means that you get even less money for what you sell.

#4: *Be prepared to sustain some loss, but not all loss.*

Distress selling seldom gets any decent margin. All you move out are your better products; then all you have left is your Chapter 11 inventory.

#5: *Don't believe that your competition has cut your price unless you can **substantiate** the fact.*

Never rely on a customer's word that "so-and-so" has a lower price. Get accurate information before taking any kind of a price cut. Is the product really being offered at the lower price, and is your competitor shipping (filling orders)at that price? Furthermore, find out if your competitor is receiving (re-stocking to sell more at that price). And, even if all the foregoing is true, is his lower price affecting your volume? There are several steps of logic that you must go through before you consider cutting price. Before you get stampeded into cutting price, *find out what's going on!*

#6: *Don't ever feel that price is either the cause of, or the solution for, a sales decline.*

A sales decline is usually caused by something other than low price -- like poor delivery, poor quality, inept marketing, or bad service.

#7: *Concentrate on the price of your total line of products rather than individual items.*

Oftentimes, someone who requires a lower price doesn't need as good merchandise as your standard product.

#8: *Consider whether you even have the **capacity** to produce more **quality** product if you do lower price and get an increase in demand.*

If you do get an increase in demand, you may not be able to ship quality product, on time (remember those volume swings associated with a price-cut). The facts are that if you do cut your price and you do get the orders, if you can't ship quality product on time, you will only antagonize your customer and what will you have gained? Don't ever forget the volume requirements that occur as a consequence of cutting price.

SUMMARY

Business is a game of margins. It is not a game of volume. All business success is sales and marketing success. Any idiot can cut price, get volume and go broke. And sales reps who sell at low prices aren't going to make any money. If your company is not making money, you aren't going to make any money either. We know that price is virtually always more significant in the mind of the seller than in the mind of the buyer, and if your price is going to be cut, it is going to be cut by *you.* Your competition does not cut your price, you do. Furthermore, it is easy to make money when you sell on some basis other than price; i.e., quality, service, delivery, advertising, promotion, salesmanship. Very few customers buy anything on price. Virtually always there are some other primary and secondary reasons for buying from a vendor. The sales rep's job is to make sure that those reasons are presented in a meaningful, useful sense to your customer.

There are two philosophical thoughts a sales rep must always retain in the back of his/her mind: (1) If price were the only reason anybody bought anything, only one vendor would sell all that is sold of it and (2) if price were the only reason that anybody bought anything, we wouldn't need sales reps.

Always remember that your customers will always tell you they buy on price, even if it is a lie, because they are trying to get *you* to cut *your* price. That is part of negotiations.

Just remember the gamesmanship of selling. A favorite story of mine, which makes this point, is one that Allan Hurst tells. Seems there was this sales rep who called on this account and, during his negotiations with the customer's purchasing agent, he noticed a quote from his major competition on the purchasing agent's desk, sitting right on top of a pile of papers. The only problem was the fact that a Coca-Cola can was sitting right on the quote. This drives the sales rep crazy, for about 10 minutes -- until the purchasing agent's phone rings. It's the boss; he wants to see the purchasing agent in his office "right now". "Yes, sir," says the purchasing agent. "I'll be right there." The purchasing agent excuses himself from the sales rep, saying "This will only take a minute or two -- seems we have a little problem -- just make yourself comfortable," and shoots out of the room.

The sales rep, of course, seizes this opportunity to lift the can of Coca-Cola to see the dollars on the quotation -- and all the B-B's in the can fly all over the room from the bottom of the can.

There are two morals to this story: (1) *Never* pick anything up off your customer's desk -- always just slide it sideways to see what is underneath, and (2) remember that *you* cut *your* price, and your customer has every right to try to get you to do so, but it is *you* who will actually do the price-cutting, not your competitor.

A

B

ORDER FORM

HORIZON PUBLICATIONS, INC.
3333 IRIS AVENUE
BOULDER, COLORADO 80301
(303) 442-8114 (800) 323-2835
FAX (303) 442-2803

PLEASE SEND ME THE FOLLOWING BOOKS AND
TAPES BY LAWRENCE L. STEINMETZ, PH.D.:

BOOKS	QTY		AMOUNT
NICE GUYS FINISH LAST (2 lbs)	_____	@ $24.95 each	_____
HOW TO SELL AT PRICES HIGHER THAN YOUR COMPETITORS (2 lbs)	_____	@ $24.95 each	_____
JENNY THE PENNY by Kelly Fano (1 lb)	_____	@ $9.95 each	_____

AUDIO TAPES	QTY		AMOUNT
MANAGING THE UNSATISFACTORY PERFORMER (6 lbs)	_____	@ $85.00 each	_____
FIRST LINE MANAGEMENT (6 lbs)	_____	@ $100.00 each	_____
MANAGING A FAST GROWING RETAIL BUSINESS (6 lbs)	_____	@ $70.00 each	_____
MANAGING A FAST GROWING MANUFACTURING COMPANY (6 lbs)	_____	@ $75.00 each	_____
HOW TO MAKE YOUR PRICES STICK (6 lbs)	_____	@ $115.00 each	_____
HOW TO SELL AT PRICES HIGHER THAN YOUR COMPETITORS (6 lbs)	_____	@ $115.00 each	_____

VIDEO TAPES	QTY		AMOUNT
HOW TO MAKE YOUR PRICES STICK PACKAGE (10 lbs)	_____	@ $800.00 each	_____
HOW TO MAKE YOUR PRICES STICK PREVIEW (includes postage)	_____	@ $15.00 each	_____
HOW TO SELL AT PRICES HIGHER THAN YOUR COMPETITORS PKG. (10 lbs)	_____	@ $800.00 each	_____
HOW TO SELL AT PRICES HIGHER THAN... PREVIEW (includes postage)	_____	@ $15.00 each	_____

---

* Continental U.S. postage based on
weight per item indicated in (lbs) after
each item.

Up to 3#	$ 4.50
4# to 9#	$ 6.75
10# to 15#	$ 9.50
over 15#	please call

(example: 2 books @ 2 lbs each = 4 lbs)

** Colorado residents only.

Sub Total _____

Postage & handling* _____

Sales Tax 6.91%** _____

TOTAL _____

PRICES SUBJECT TO CHANGE
ALL SALES FINAL

☐ Check Enclosed

Charge To:
☐ American Express
☐ Master Card
☐ Visa

Send To _____

Company Name _____

Street Address _____

City _____ State _____ Zip _____

Phone Number _____

Card Number _____ Exp. Date _____

Name on Card _____

Signature _____